▲▲

Amazing
Secrets of
the Mystic East

▲▲

Also by the Author:

Norvell's Dynamic Mental Laws for Successful Living

Meta-Physics: New Dimensions of the Mind

Cosmic Magnetism: The Miracle of the Magic Power Circle

Mind Cosmology

The Occult Sciences: How to Get What You Want Through Your Occult Powers

The Miracle Power of Transcendental Meditation

The $100,000 Dream and How to Make it Come True

Money Magnetism: How to Grow Rich Beyond Your Wildest Dreams

Universal Secrets of Telecosmic Power

The Oriental 7-Day Quick Weight-Off Diet

Alpha-Psychics: Mystic Path to Perfect Living

Mystical Power of Universal Healing

▲
AMAZING
▲▲▲
SECRETS OF
▲▲▲▲▲
THE MYSTIC EAST
▲▲▲▲▲▲▲

by

NORVELL

Parker Publishing Company, Inc.
West Nyack, New York

© 1980 *by*

PARKER PUBLISHING COMPANY, INC.

West Nyack, N.Y.

Library of Congress Cataloging in Publication Data

Norvell.
    Amazing secrets of the mystic East.

    1. Success. 2. Occult sciences.
I. Title.
BJ1611.2.N623   131'.3   79-19800
ISBN 0-13-023754-X

Printed in the United States of America

DEDICATION

I gratefully dedicate this book to the million and a half students who have studied these mystic secrets from the East with me in my many years of lecturing at world-famous Carnegie Hall. To the students who have come to study with me from all over the world, I owe my inspiration to continue in this work that has brought all of us so much joy and enlightenment.

Norvell

WHAT THIS BOOK
WILL DO FOR YOU

In your mystical quest for greater wisdom and knowledge you must travel back through time and space into the unlimited domain of mystic revelations from India, Tibet, China and Egypt. Some of the greatest secrets of all time have been revealed by the mystics, seers, prophets and teachers who lived in those ancient days.

In this book, you will learn how you can apply their dynamic secrets of mysticism to modern twentieth-century living for greater power. You will be shown how to command and control the hidden forces of the universe and achieve the fulfillment of your every dream.

During your journey you will not only go to the Far East where mysticism was born, but you will also learn some of the great secrets from the Middle East, particularly Egypt, where this knowledge was used to build one of the greatest civilizations ever known to man.

POTENT PYRAMID POWER CAN
BE YOURS FOR WORKING
MIRACLES

What you will study about the pyramids alone can help you unlock vast reservoirs of spiritual power that can truly make you a miracle worker. You will use pyramid power to regenerate your body and keep it healthy and young, to overcome sickness and be healthy and vital, to achieve your life goals, to build a vast fortune and have everything in life that you ever dreamed of having.

When you once master the ancient mystical secrets that you will study in this book, your life will be one of effortless ease. In just a few moments a day, in the privacy of your own home, without effort of any kind, you will be able to use the mystic meditations, chants and mantras that are given to tap a higher intelligence in the universe which can motivate your life in any direction you may choose.

7

45 MYSTICAL SECRETS
THAT WILL INSTANTLY
TRANSFORM YOUR LIFE

1.   Learn how to use Tibetan White Magic Rituals to literally perform miracles of healing, accumulate wealth and live to be one hundred years of age more. Rita R. suffered from chronic illness, bronchial asthma and sinus infection and was healed completely by using Tibetan White Magic. See Chapter 3.

2.   Discover the invisible world of psychic phenomena and learn how you can use this power to guide you in your life. Jennie L. projected her perfect soul mate and was guided by psychic vision to finding the ideal man. Her story is told in Chapter 4.

3.   From the ancient land of India, you will be given the Golden Midas Touch that was used by the Maharajahs of that fabled land to build their vast fortunes. Cyrus D. and his wife used this secret method of psychic projection and attracted a business that brought them $50,000. This secret is revealed in Chapter 2.

4.   Find out about the mystical power of Kundalini to give you life energy and health. Douglas J. healed a heart condition by using this mystic power. See chapter 9 to learn more about this miraculous power.

5.   Learn how you can overcome black magic with white magic that can instantly change your life. Wilma K. was nearly destroyed by black magic forces until she learned of this mystical power. Her story is told in Chapter 3.

6.   Loretta J. used the Pyramid Blue Print of Destiny to develop a business worth more than $100,000 a year. Discover this secret in Chapter 1.

7.   Mysteries of the I Ching can make you a living Oracle that foresees your destiny. Sara L. consulted the I Ching and discovered a secret will that brought her a $125,000 inheritance. See Chapter 14.

8.   There are four stages of Mysticism which you can use to literally perform miracles in your life. Therese H. had mental and physical problems which she overcame by using mystic chants and meditations. This is revealed in Chapter 5.

9.   Learn how you can use the Mystical Money Mantra to attract as much money as you desire. Marvin P., a salesman, used this money mantra and doubled his sales in a few days. See Chapter 7.

10.   You can release Pyramid Power to help you overcome bad habits and live a healthy, happy life. Daryl J. smoked for 15 years and stopped within two weeks through this secret. See Chapter 7 to learn how he did this.

11.   Cosmic Magnetism can be released in your life through the mystical Yin-Yang system from ancient China. See how Linda D. used the Yang qualities to win a husband at 45 years of age. This is given in Chapter 11.

12.   Do you believe that you have lived before? In Chapter 10, you will discover the method for knowing your past lives. Laura G. used this knowledge to reveal an ancient Egyptian incarnation.

13.   Find out how you can open your psychic third eye to perceive amazing revelations. Richard W. had a clairvoyant vision and was told what stock to buy. He made thousands of dollars! See how he did this in Chapter 4.

14.   Discover how you can switch on the Mysto-Psychic screen within your higher mind and have astounding visions of future events. Susan E. used this method to win a $50,000 lottery. See Chapter 13. Others have used this method to win from $10,000. to $100,000.

15.   Learn about the Mystical Money Press that you can literally use to project large sums of money when you need it. Viola K. used this money press to bring her a new career and more money than she ever thought possible. This method is revealed in Chapter 13.

16.   You will be taken into the Pyramid Initiation mystery in Chapter 1, that gives you regeneration and rebirth. When you use this initiation ceremony you will have astounding power. Donald W. built a million dollar business after his Initiation.

17.   What are Psycho-Astral Rays? You will be shown, in Chapter 15, how the mystics from beyond the Himalayas used this mystical power to project mental images to the outer world. Pearl H. used these Psycho-Astral Rays to project her ideal soul mate after two failures in marriage.

18.   Deborah L. had serious sexual problems with her husband. She studied about the Chakra that controls reproduction and was able to overcome this problem. See Chapter 9 for this information.

19.   Discover the millionaire's secret vow that can help you build a fortune. This is given in Chapter 2. Martha A., a nurse, used this power and opened a nursing home with a retired doctor and made a fortune.

20.   Learn how you can use the Seven Mystical Stages of Yoga to give you control of your mind and body. Desmond P. felt old and useless and overcame severe illness and old age through Yoga practices. This full Yoga regime is given to you in Chapter 9.

21.   There is a mystical Ritual from the Pyramids which can give you the ability to project large sums of money. See how Mary Lou F. used this Pyramid

Ritual to attract $125,000 in the most mysterious manner. This information will be given to you in Chapter 1.

22.   Mr. and Mrs. T.R. wanted to have their own Dream Home. They tapped the invisible world of psychic phenomena, as given in Chapter 4, and they were guided to finding the perfect home.

23.   Can you believe that a ritual of Psychic Meditation can cause a person to lose from 10 to 50 pounds of weight? Morton E. was 40 pounds overweight and used the information given in Chapter 5 to lose 40 pounds in a short time.

24.   Discover for yourself the secret mystical practice known as Samyama that gives you astounding power. Pamela S. was considered an ugly duckling and changed herself into the proverbial swan through this method of Samyama. Find out about this power in Chapter 13.

25.   There are Astral Planes that you can explore while you sleep. Secrets are given to you on these Astral planes that profoundly affect your life. Wanda E. had an astral dream of a fire and was able to save her husband's life. See how this power can be tapped in Chapter 15.

26.   Bernice E. wanted a beautiful mink coat, and through an amazing psychic revelation, she was given a gift of a $5,000 coat! Learn how to use this psychic projection in Chapter 4.

27.   Learn how you may use the Psychic Mirror practice in the revelations from ancient India, and come into a cycle of prosperity and good fortune. Bruce T. used this mirror practice and was soon selling double the number of houses he had formerly sold. This method is revealed in Chapter 6.

28.   There are seven Creative Astral rays revealed in the Pyramid Mysteries of ancient Egypt. Helen F. tapped this creative power and attracted the sum of $35,000 in a health food business. The release of this Pyramid power is given in Chapter 7.

29.   There is a mystical Law of Mental Alchemy that you can use to change your destiny. In Chapter 8 you will find out how to find the mystical pathway to heaven that brings you freedom from earth's hinderances.

30.   There are mystical rites in the Temple of Osiris in ancient Egypt that release tremendous healing power. Gertrude D. was very sick, and by using the ritual of sun and moon blending, she had a complete miracle healing. Chapter 7 gives these healings rituals.

31.   One of the most amazing mystical secrets from India is that of the Psycho-Radar screen which can protect you from all danger. This works like a real radar in life and gives you warnings of danger. Study this method in Chapter 13.

32.   Do you know the 15 sources of trouble in life and how to avoid them? Confucius in ancient China revealed this knowledge to be found in Chapter 8. Josephine A. found out her husband was unfaithful and tried to kill him. See how she was saved from utter ruination.

33.   Discover the Yin-Yang diet from the mysticism of the Far East, and see the amazing results in better health and longer life. In Chapter 11, you will be given this previously hidden knowledge.

34.   Have you ever lost something you could not find? Or have you wanted to find a gold mine, and oil well or hidden water? There is a method revealed in Chapter 4, which tells you how to find these things. Fred J. discovered an abandoned gold mine that yielded $35,000. Sybil S. found an engagement ring that she had lost.

35.   From an ancient buried monastery at the foot of the Himalayas, I discovered a Tibetan secret that literally works miracles and that can give you peace of mind and soul serenity. Learn how you can ascend to the spiritual mountaintop and find your Shangri-la in Chapter 3.

36.   There are seven mystical chakras that you will find revealed through a study of Ancient Yoga. You can open these seven chakras through a process of meditation that you will find in Chapter 9.

37.   The Egyptian Flame Ritual from the Pyramids gives you the ability to release tremendous miracle working power. Through this Flame Ritual Burton T. overcame drug dependence. Tyrone G. projected a yacht, in the flame ritual and he got it in a short time. This ritual is given in Chapter 12.

38.   Learn how to use Psychic Reverie to project pictures of the money or things you want onto a psychic screen like on your TV set. Rosita E. wanted an $800 color TV set but only had $100. See how she got it through Psychic Reverie in Chapter 4.

39.   The exercise of Mystical Moon Blending was used by the Ancients to take on magical qualities in the Aura. Dorothy B. used this secret to change her life. She attracted a young doctor who proposed marriage. Find out about Moon Blending in Chapter 7.

40.   Why are some people born rich and destined to fame while others are born poor and unlucky? There is an Akashic record and Karmic Birthpath revealed in Chapter 10 that explains this mystery. See how Linda C. read her Akashic record and how it helped her in life.

41.   Adele F. found that her husband was under a black magic spell from another woman. Learn how she broke this evil force with a ritual of the Flame and won back her husband's love. See Chapter 12.

42.   When Harold C. wanted to change his work from plumbing to landscape gardening and horticulture, everyone told him it was impossible. Read how he used the secret forces of Yin-Yang to completely revolutionize his life. This is revealed in Chapter 11.

43.   Discover the Noble Eightfold Path to greatness and achievement which the Buddha revealed in Ancient India. Rita Y. had a retarded son and a lifetime of misfortunes but she overcame the pain of suffering by using this secret principle given in Chapter 6.

44.   Can your soul contact the soul of the universe and have the knowledge of the ages? Miracles are possible when you use the four stages of mysticism to achieve this spiritual elevation. Agatha C. was ruining her life with tranquilizers and pep pills, until she learned how to use meditation to contact the soul of the universe. This amazing story is given in Chapter 5.

45.   Ten of life's greatest treasures are yours to have when you once release mystic power. Clarice J. wanted the treasure of true love and projected her ideal soul mate through this method. Howard R. wanted to become a factory foreman and have a bigger salary. He used the method given in detail in Chapter 13 and achieved his goal. Also learn in this chapter, how to use Psychic Somnambulism to overcome life's tradgedies and have perpetual joy and peace.

The wonderful thing about the application of this eastern wisdom is the speed with which you get results—often instantaneous, automatic results—at most a few days', or weeks' time. So start your personal program using the methods that have benefited mankind for eons. Listen to the voices of ancient sages and seers from the Far East as they guide you to a far richer life than you ever imagined possible.

NORVELL

CONTENTS

The Tapestry of Timeless Wisdom • Miracles Performed by Great Mystics of the Past • Ask for a Miracle Today • Mysterious Pyramid Power Will Transform Your Life • The Fantastic Lore of Egyptian Mysteries Revealed • Pyramid Energy Can Bring You Riches and Abundance • Testimony No. 1—Donald W. Built a Million Dollar Business Through Pyramid Power • Potent Pyramid Power Revealed in the King's Chamber • Step-by-Step Instructions for Your Initiation Into the Deeper Mysteries • Dedication Ceremony for Regeneration and Rebirth • How to Release Pranic Power Through Your Breath • Dedication Ceremony for Greater Energy and Vital Good Health • Write Down All the Things You Desire for Greater Concentration of Power • Testimony No. 2—Loretta J. Gets $100,000 Through the Pyramid Blueprint • Testimony No. 3—Fern L. Heals Herself With Pyramid Power • The Pyramid Form Releases Cosmic Energy and Power • Cure Headaches With Pyramid Energy • Pyramid Power to Help You Avoid Accidents While Driving • Testimony No. 4—Pyramid Power Protected Edward T. • How to Release Pyramid Energy to Attract Large Sums of

Books, Art and Music Give Pleasure • Enjoy the Beauty in Nature and the Changing Seasons • Live in the World of Natural Splendor • Pave Your Pathway to Paradise With the Golden Dream of Love's Sweet Ecstasy • Use the Mystical Law of Mental Alchemy to Change the Negative Conditions of Life Into Positive Ones • How to Use the Law of Mental Alchemy to Change Your Life • Build Mental and Spiritual Values and Rise Above the Materialistic Realm to Find True Lasting Happiness • Lao-Tse's Pathway to Heaven • Mysto-Matic Pointers

How to Release the Mystical Power of Kundalini for Life Energy • How to Achieve the State of Hatha Yoga for Vital Good Health • How to Assume the Lotus Position for Meditation • The Sacred Mantra—Aum Mane Padme Aum— for Meditation • The Seven Mystical Centers, or Chakras, of Yoga • How to Activate the Seven Chakras and Open the Padmas • Testimony No. 38—Desmond P. Overcame Illness and Depression Due to Age • How to Achieve the State of Laya Yoga for Quiescence • Meditation for Achieving the State of Laya Yoga • Testimony No. 39—How Deborah L. Used Laya Yoga to Achieve Inner Peace • Sexual Difficulties Can Be Overcome Through Use of Yoga Exercises • Meditation to Help Overcome the Problem of Frigidity in Sex • How to Achieve the State of Mantra Yoga for Psychic Power • Meditation for Achieving the State of Mantra Yoga • How to Achieve the State of Bhakti Yoga for Spiritual Ecstasy • Meditation for Achieving the State of Bhakti Yoga for Spiritual Ecstasy • Bhakti Yoga Can Be Used to Heal Heart Conditions • Testimony No. 40— Douglas J. Used Bhakti Yoga to Heal a Heart Condition • Yoga Meditation for Healing a Heart Condition • How to Achieve the State of Karma Yoga for Mental, Physical and Spiritual Balance • Meditation for Achieving Karma Yoga for Balance • How to Achieve the State of Jnana Yoga for Spiritual Growth • Meditation for Achieving the State of Jnana Yoga • How to Activate the Sixth Chakra for Spiritual

*to Help You Build Yang Qualities of Magnetism • Yang
Meditation to Help You Face Life's Challenges • How You Can
Acquire the Yang Qualities of Leadership and Superior-
ity • Testimony No. 45—How a Young Plumber Used the
Power of Yang to Choose a New Career • How to Build the Yang
Quality of Optimism in Your Personality • How to Use the
Oriental System of Yin-Yang for Peace of Mind • Yang
Meditation to Help You Acquire Riches and Fulfillment of
Destiny • The Yin-Yang Foods for Health and Long
Life • Mysto-Matic Pointers*

*A Scientist Caused Warts to Disappear by Using the Flame
Ritual • Your Mind Can Release a Curse or a Bless-
ing • Regimen for Using the Sacred Egyptian Flame Ritual to
Make Your Dreams Come True • Write Down Your Requests
for the Sacred Flame • Testimony No. 46—How Tyrone G.
Projected a Yacht in the Flame Ritual • Use the Flame Ritual to
Turn Black Magic Forces Into White Magic Forces • Testimony
No. 47—How Adele F. Broke an Evil Spell With the Flame
Ritual • How to Use White Magic to Influence Others for
Good • Black Magic Forces Destroyed Hundreds at
Guyana • Testimony No. 48—Raymond R. Used the Flame
Ritual to Get Back Money He Loaned • How to Use the Flame
Ritual for Healing Sickness • Testimony No. 49—Edith F. Used
the Flame Ritual to Avoid Surgery • Use the Flame Ritual to
Overcome Habits of Smoking or Alcoholism • Testimony No.
50—Burton T. Overcame Drug Dependence With the Flame
Ritual • Mysto-Matic Pointers*

*Treasure No. 1—Divine Guidance Through Inner
Perception • How to Switch on the Mysto-Psychic Screen Within*

▲▲▲▲▲▲▲▲▲▲▲▲▲▲▲▲▲▲▲▲▲▲▲▲▲▲▲▲▲▲▲▲▲▲▲▲▲▲▲

Amazing
Secrets of
the Mystic East

▲▲▲▲▲▲▲▲▲▲▲▲▲▲▲▲▲▲▲▲▲▲▲▲▲▲▲▲▲▲▲▲▲▲▲▲▲▲▲

1

DISCOVER THE SECRETS OF THE MYSTIC EAST— AND START LIVING

You were born into one of the greatest mysteries of all time. Your soul was projected into a vital, living body, with a creative thinking brain that shares in the mystery called "Life."

Did you ever stop to question the reason for your being in this world, sharing in these magnificent life experiences, enjoying the excitement of love, the adventure of discovery and the creation of the miracle of new life?

Can the true purpose behind your life be one of mere sensual enjoyment, animal appetites, the search for money, power, fame and fortune? Or is there a deeper, more mystical reason why you were born?

THE TAPESTRY OF TIMELESS
WISDOM

This tapestry of timeless wisdom that comes to us from the Far East and the Middle East, which tries to comprehend and chart the invisible forces of life, is called Mysticism.

Some of the greatest revelations of all time have come to us from the mystical lands of ancient India, China, Tibet and Egypt. These deeper mysteries have spread throughout the world, laying the foundations upon which civilization was built.

Some of these great truths spread to Greece and influenced the philosophers of that ancient land. They were to be found in ancient Japan and laid the foundations for Shintoism and Buddhism. They became a part of the wisdom of Jerusalem, which comprised the background of the ancient Jewish faith, and ushered in the Christian dispensation. Moses's laws of the Ten Commandments and Jesus's Golden Rule and Sermon on the Mount have permeated the laws and educational systems upon which our Western civilization has been built.

MIRACLES PERFORMED BY
GREAT MYSTICS OF THE PAST

The great mystics like Moses, Abraham and Jesus used some of these revelations which caused them to perform miracles in their time. Turning a stick into a crawling serpent, or changing water into wine, walking on the water, healing the sick, all these miraculous forces showed the use of ancient white magic and transcendental spiritual forces that came directly from the mystical lands of India, China, Tibet and Egypt. In fact, the teachings of the Far East and Mid-East preceded the teachings of the Christian mystic, Jesus, by several hundred years!

ASK FOR A MIRACLE TODAY

You can become a part of this great cosmic scheme of mysticism and ask for your own personal miracle today. You can use the forces of occultism, white magic, invocations, rituals, chants and meditations to release the creative energy of your own higher nature and perform miracles in your own life.

In this chapter, I will relate to you the secret initiation ceremony performed in the King's Chamber in the vast Pyramid of Giza. This secret that came to the mid-eastern country of Egypt originated in the teachings of the great masters of India and Tibet. You will learn the secrets of regeneration for your mind and body and discover the new self-image that gives you power and command over the invisible forces of life. You will learn how the Initiates into these deeper mysteries literally died to the old life and were reborn in mind, body and spirit.

MYSTERIOUS PYRAMID POWER
WILL TRANSFORM YOUR LIFE

Even today, modern scientists are baffled by the mysteries contained in the Pyramids of Egypt. They now believe that the ancient Egyptians were able to tap some secret, mystical power that caused them to build the three pyramids in Egypt, which are so complicated that even modern scientists would not be able to duplicate them.

The Egyptians believed in the continuity of life. They also believed in reincarnation, the belief that the soul has lived before and will live again. They prepared for the mystical experience of death as much as they did for life. They symbolically prepared a small boat to carry the departed one's soul into the journey into eternity. They filled the tombs of their kings and queens with various foods, personal jewelry and clothing, preparing them for the mystical journey into the unknown.

THE FANTASTIC LORE OF
EGYPTIAN MYSTERIES REVEALED

The recent discoveries of the priceless treasures and works of art in King Tutankhamen's tomb cause modern scientists to realize that the ancient Egyptians indeed possessed amazing super-normal powers that created one of the greatest civilizations of all time.

You will now learn how to use this miracle-working power for your own purposes, not only to achieve a complete rebirth mentally, physically and spiritually, but to actually tap Pyramid Power for healing your body, if you should ever become sick.

You will discover a secret key for attuning your higher mind centers to the great cosmic intelligence that rules the universe, so that you can find peace of mind and peace of soul.

This knowledge from ancient Egypt will help bring you fulfillment in love and marriage, for you will learn how to use the cosmic wavelengths of mystical power like a giant magnet which can attract your true soul mate into your orbit of life experience.

PYRAMID ENERGY CAN BRING
YOU RICHES AND ABUNDANCE

Pyramid Energy can bring you riches and abundance. You can project your dreams and aspirations upon a cosmic wavelength attuned to success and your life will suddenly blossom with priceless treasures—gold and silver, jewels and houses and lands, modern cars and household appliances, color TV sets, all the appurtenances of modern living can be yours when you unlock this tremendous mystical power that caused the Pyramids to be created in such majestic and unbelievable proportions!

Testimony No. 1

Donald W. Built a Million Dollar Business Through Pyramid Power

An instance of how this mystical power of the Pyramids can be used to bring wealth was that of a student of mine named Donald W. He wanted to be rich so he could give his children a fine education, he longed to live in a beautiful home, drive an expensive car, and have financial security for the future. He had a good job making a fair salary but when he learned about these mysteries of the pyramids he suddenly had an expanded vision and an intense desire to be more successful and have a fortune.

Each day, Donald sat in quiet meditation, using the exact instructions I am now going to reveal for you to use, and one day he had a sudden intuitive flash of inspiration that he could use the same mystical power the ancient Egyptians did when they conceived the impossible task of building the Pyramids! Donald knew, in that inspiring moment, that the same power exists in the world today and that he could also tap it to build a great destiny.

A sudden inspiration came through to him: Dream big! The words were written out in letters of gold on his Psychic Mental screen as he sat in meditation. As Donald was working for an electronics firm, he suddenly had the inspiration that electronics are the new age revelation in the form of computers, recorders, video and tape machines, air conditioning and solar energy, atomic power and space travel. Why not form a company that will furnish such new-age equipment to the world?

In an amazingly short time, Donald met a rich man who was willing to put up the initial money to form such a company and they were soon heading a million dollar business—with Donald as President!

POTENT PYRAMID POWER
REVEALED IN THE KING'S
CHAMBER

I can attest to the miraculous powers that can be released through our higher mind centers when we are initiated into the deeper Pyramid mysteries. I am one of the few modern men to have spent an entire night in the great pyramid of Giza. In the pyramid, I experienced some of the most startling revelations of my entire life.

I had a battery operated tape recorder with me, and as I sat there in the very heart of the Pyramid, I went into a deep trance and some power spoke through me that revealed some of the ancient pyramid secrets known only to the great souls who built it.

I was given the actual ritual and invocation used by the ancient Egyptians in the initiation ceremony of regeneration and rebirth. This ritual, that I am now going to share with you, will help elevate you to a plane of cosmic consciousness where you are instantly given miracle working powers.

STEP-BY-STEP INSTRUCTIONS
FOR YOUR INITIATION INTO
THE DEEPER MYSTERIES

1.   To prepare yourself for the ceremony of regeneration and rebirth, seek out a quiet place where you will not be disturbed. Have a white candle lit and some incense burning. Lie down in a comfortable position on your bed. This will duplicate the exact position taken by the neophyte in the granite sarcophagus that is in the King's chamber of the Pyramid of Giza.

2.   If you can obtain a miniature pyramid made of wood, metal or plastic, it will help you concentrate this pyramid power in your higher mind centers. However, even if you do not have such a pyramid form in your room, you can duplicate this through spiritual and occult means in your own consciousness by visualizing the giant pyramid in Egypt and holding it in your consciousness as you do this initiation ceremony.

DEDICATION CEREMONY FOR
REGENERATION AND REBIRTH

3.   Now you are ready for the actual dedication and initiation ceremony that will give you the power to achieve any goal in life that you desire. You will now go through the process of rebirth and regeneration which will give you a tremendous awareness of your own great spiritual powers to create the world you desire.

Read the following dedication statement quietly, to yourself:

I am now an initiate into the deeper mysteries of the great brotherhood of light. I lay aside my cloak of mortality and take on the immortal raiment of my soul's true illumination and immortality.

I am now reborn in consciousness and I become a channel through which the higher cosmic forces can work for me, to bring me the things that I desire in life.

HOW TO RELEASE PRANIC
POWER THROUGH YOUR
BREATH

4.   Now you will be aware of your breath. Breathe deeply to the count of four, hold the breath for a few moments and then release it slowly. Do this about ten times, as you now say to yourself:

I now dedicate my breath as a living prayer of thanksgiving for the gift of life. My breath ascends to the celestial heights, linking me to the Cosmic Power that rules the universe.

My mind and body are now attuned to Cosmic Power. This healing force animates my mind, my body and my soul with the desire to live and express power. I am being healed by this celestial ray and I express life, health, power, youth and joy.

DEDICATION CEREMONY FOR
GREATER ENERGY AND VITAL
GOOD HEALTH

5.   As the next step in your initiation into the deeper Pyramid mysteries, be aware of your body. This is the chalice through which Cosmic Mind works to create your good in life. Now breathe deeply again for ten counts and exhale, saying the following dedication:

> *I dedicate my body as a channel through which Cosmic Power flows. I am imbued with creative emotions of joy, peace, goodness and love. I express my creative gifts to benefit and enrich the world.*
>
> *I now dedicate my mind as a channel for creativity. I receive illumination from the spiritual heights that can transform my life and bring me riches and abundance. I lay aside all concepts of inferiority, limitation and age, as I am now reborn in consciousness. I am being purified of all negative and destructive forces. I control my mind and my emotions. I am worthy of the best that life has to offer and I now petition the higher cosmic forces to grant me the following treasures and gifts:*
>
> *I wish to become more spiritually aware so that my true destiny will be revealed to me.*
>
> *I desire a physically perfect body which shall be maintained in good health for one hundred years or more.*
>
> *I ask for guidance from my higher psychic mind centers, so I can overcome my problems and know peace and tranquility.*
>
> *I wish to be given creative gifts and talents through which I can find my right place in the business world.*
>
> *I desire love/happiness with my true soul mate and ask that I shall find this perfect mate soon.*
>
> *I wish to have large sums of money so I may give my family all the essentials and comforts of life.*
>
> *I desire a home of my own, in which my family and myself can know security, peace and joy.*
>
> *I wish to become more patient and loving, so I can attract friends who will admire, respect and love me.*

WRITE DOWN ALL THE THINGS
YOU DESIRE FOR GREATER
CONCENTRATION OF POWER

6.   You may not be able to actually remember all of the above requests you wish to make of the higher Cosmic Intelligence, as you go through your dedication ceremony, so I suggest that you write down all the things you wish to have granted to you. You can put down actual sums of money, such as $5,000 or $10,000.

Testimony No. 2.

Loretta J. Gets $100,000 Through the Pyramid Blueprint

Loretta J. was one of my lecture members in Los Angeles, who had a real need for a large sum of money; she had been left a widow, with two teen-aged children to care for and educate. She wrote down on her Pyramid Blueprint for the future: I desire the sum of $100,000 to give my children and myself overall security for the future. She did the entire dedication ceremony, as given above, several times over a period of four weeks before she had results. Loretta had an Aunt who had built a big business in San Fernando Valley, in ceramics and statuary. She and her husband had built the business to a point where it was making more then $100,000 a year. When her husband died, Loretta had asked her widowed Aunt if she could help in the business. For two years she worked hard to learn the entire business. One day, after Loretta had done her initiation ceremony again, her aunt called her into the office and told her, "You've worked hard to help me with the business. Now I'm old and tired and I want to take a trip around the world. I'm turning the business over to you and only ask that you give me one third of the proceeds for my living expenses." This was a true miracle, for there were other relatives the aunt could have given the business to and Loretta is convinced that her Pyramid Rituals did the work of persuading her aunt to give her the successful business. Now Loretta lives in a beautiful home in the valley, her children are assured of a good education, and she has already found her true soul mate and is on the way to a happy marriage!

7.   If you should have some actual physical illness that you wish to treat through this initiation ceremony you can obtain a healing of your ailment by using the following meditation:

> *I now lay aside my old mortal mind concepts of age and sickness. I am reborn in the new consciousness of health, vital energy and long life. I now petition the higher cosmic forces to renew every cell and atom of my brain and body with life energy and vitality. I ask that I become healed of this illness and that my body shall become healed*

perfectly for all time. I now set my cosmic time clock to one hundred years of zestful, healthful, vibrant living.

Testimony No. 3

Fern L. Heals Herself With Pyramid Power

Fern L. had suffered for years with many forms of illness, and doctors did not seem able to help her. Fern had not been able to eat and digest her food for some years. She had colitis and suffered from constant pain in the lower intestines. She tried every known form of diet and finally the doctors gave up as she did not respond to any form of medication. The doctors wanted to do an exploratory operation on Fern and that's when she sought out our work.

In my first interview with Fern I told her about the miracles that had been performed by Pyramid Power. Out of the seventy people who had visited the Pyramids with me and who had learned how to perform the initiation cermony in the King's Chamber, many of them had worked miracles in their own lives.

I told Fern about one woman who had been barren and unable to concieve a child previously. After the Pyramid Ceremony she became pregnant in two months! Another person, a man who had a severe heart condition, was completely healed. This gave Fern faith in the miracle working power of the ceremony in the Pyramid, so she entered into the rituals with great enthusiasm.

In Fern's case I directed her to visualize a golden ball of light shining through her higher mind into the lower parts of her body as she intoned the following healing meditation:

I now direct the healing ray of golden pyramid power to my stomach and intestines. This higher power is now healing my body and bringing me perfect health. I relax my mind and body, I breathe deeply of the pranic healing life force and send it down into my body organs. I am now being healed, healed, healed.

It took Fern two weeks of daily meditation, using this regeneration ceremony, to completely heal herself. When she returned to the doctors for X-rays and examination, they were surprised to find she was healed! They called it a miracle.

THE PYRAMID FORM RELEASES
COSMIC ENERGY AND POWER

8.   The Pyramid shape itself has been claimed by modern scientists to focus some kind of cosmic energy that can actually perform miracles. It has been found that meat can be left in a pyramid shaped object for days without spoiling. Dull razor blades, when exposed to pyramid energy have been resharpened and can be used many times. Dynamic energy and youthful vitality seem to be released through the mystical properties of the Pyramid form, and some people today are keeping a small pyramid under their beds while they sleep. They report they awaken with greater energy and vitality. A famous silent movie star who is eighty years of age, admitted recently that she sleeps with a pyramid under her bed and she attributes her remarkable youthful appearance and vital energy to this fact.

CURE HEADACHES WITH
PYRAMID ENERGY

9.   If you can obtain some small pyramids made of metal, wood, or even cardboard, you can begin to use them in the following manner. When you have a headache or any other pain, place the small pyramid on the forehead or wherever the pain is located. Leave it there for about five minutes and intone this invocation.

> *I now direct Pyramid power to my body, asking the higher cosmic forces to remove all sensation of pain. I now relax and let this cosmic energy flow through my mind and body, bringing me instant healing and freedom from pain.*

PYRAMID POWER TO HELP
YOU AVOID ACCIDENTS WHILE
DRIVING

10.   Keep a Pyramid somewhere in your car when driving. It can be on the back seat or in the rear window, where it is a constant focal point of protec-

tive power. It helps deflect danger, it mobilizes your energies and makes you more relaxed and responsive in your reflexes, so you can avoid accidents.

Testimony No. 4

Pyramid Power Protected Edward T.

Edward T. had a Pyramid shape made of metal that he carried constantly in his car for three months. The reason for this was that he had previously had three accidents, seemingly through no fault of his own. He learned in our classes about Pyramid power protection and he began to carry his protective pyramid in the car.

In the three-month period that he reported to me, he did not have a single accident! He drove with more confidence and he believed that the pyramid shape sent out some kind of cosmic energy that helped him be a more alert driver.

HOW TO RELEASE PYRAMID ENERGY TO ATTRACT LARGE SUMS OF MONEY

11.   To begin the flow of money into your life, you can use a small pyramid to concentrate on. Sit before this pyramid and look at it, giving yourself the pyramid money treatment. You will notice that on our American dollar bill, on the green side there is a picture of a pyramid within a circle, with an eye in the very top of the pyramid. This occult symbol relates to the spiritual energy that is given out by a higher power which translates things and ideas into currency.

Sit in meditation and look at a small pyramid as you intone the following Money Meditation.

> *I now project Pyramid Money Power to my higher psychic mind centers. I ask for creative ideas to be released to my mind that can make me rich. I project the sum of $10,000 on my psychic screen and ask that I be guided to making that money from unexpected sources.*

You can actually project sums of $500, $5,000 or $50,000 or more, depending on your needs. Keep up this money pyramid projection for at least a month or more, until you are able to begin your demonstration of sums of money you require to bring you security.

TestimonyNo. 5.

Mary Lou F. Receives an Unexpected Inheritance

Mary Lou F. was a New York lecture member who had severe money problems. At one of our classes I gave the students the above Pyramid Money ritual and told them to begin projecting sums of money they thought they needed for overall security.

Mary Lou started asking for $125,000. She told me that if she had that amount she would have financial security the rest of her life. She had a real need since her husband had left her with two small children, and she had to go on welfare to take care of them.

Mary Lou had an old aunt who lived in a squalid walk-up apartment in the ghetto districts of New York. Whenever she could, Mary Lou would visit the old lady, bringing her food and giving her comfort. The old aunt was constantly sick, and without heat or help of any kind.

After Mary Lou had performed her Pyramid Money ritual for about two months, she was surprised when a policeman came to her door with very distressing news. Her aunt had been found dead in her apartment, the victim of malnutrition and bitter cold. A few days later, after Mary Lou had borrowed money for her aunt's funeral, she received word from a lawyer that the police had found hidden in her aunt's apartment $125,000 in securities and cash! As there was no other relative, this entire estate went to Mary Lou! What mysterious cosmic currents caused Mary Lou to tune in to the exact sum of $125,000 that her aunt had hidden? She believed that this was due to the mystical power released by her Pyramid Money Ritual.

MYSTO-MATIC POINTERS

1. *You can go into the initiation ceremony of the Pyramids to ask for information about your past reincarnations. By putting yourself into a semi-trance through deep breathing and concentration, you can summon up a review of past lives to see why you suffer in this lifetime.*

> *Then you can set about correcting the Karmic mistakes you have made in the past.*

2. *Each night when you prepare for sleep, you can enter into the initiation ceremony, giving your higher mind instructions to work on healing your body all night long. In this way you can avoid most of life's illnesses.*

3. *If you have problems that seem unsolvable you can sit in meditation before a pyramid form and direct your higher mind as follows: Help me solve this problem immediately. I now ask for psychic guidance to my right course of action.*

4. *Make out a list of your desires that you carry into your pyramid meditation sessions. Write them out in detail; read them every morning and every night, and then as different things come true, scratch them out and write new ones.*

5. *All during the day, remember your dedication breath, which is a living prayer, and repeat, several times a day:*

I breathe deeply of the pranic life force. I direct it to my body cells to heal me all day long of any afflictions. My breath is now purifying my mind and body with cosmic life energy and pyramid power.

6. *As you look at the Pyramid on the back of the dollar bill, concentrate on the eye at the peak of the pyramid and intone:*

I now open my psychic third eye so that I may have divine guidance all day today. I am aware of the magic circle of God's protective love and I shall be safe and secure all day long.

7. *Each morning, when you awaken, give yourself the following Pyramid regeneration invocation:*

I am reborn in every cell of my brain and body. I now feel the surging of new life energy and cosmic power within my body and I become rejuvenated, reinvigorated, refreshed and reborn.

8. *Be sure that you awaken each morning with an awareness of the cosmic flow of energy through your breathing. Make it a point to breathe deeply ten times,*

holding the breath a few seconds, then releasing it saying:

Thank you God for another day of life, in which I dedicate my breath as a living prayer of thanksgiving to your greater glory. All day today, as I breathe, my breath shall ascend as a living prayer to the celestial heights.

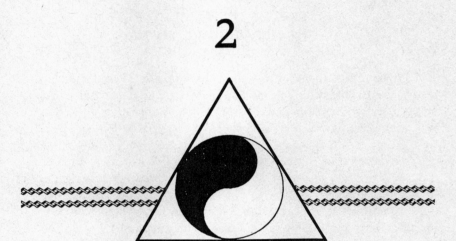

2

TRIGGER THE GOLDEN MIDAS TOUCH FROM INDIA FOR ASTOUNDING RICHES AND ABUNDANCE

From ancient India there comes a great mystical power that can bring you riches and abundance. The India of today is totally different from the India of the past when Maharajahs ruled and accumulated vast treasures from all over the world.

These rulers of India were instructed in the Mystical arts of that vast continent by great masters or Gurus, some of them travelling to India from Tibet.

By using these mystical revelations for accumulating wealth, you can apply the same rules that made these Maharajahs fabulously rich. They possessed the greatest collections of gold and silver the world has even known. In their palace vaults, they stored huge quantities of diamonds, rubies, emeralds, sapphires and pearls. These learned Maharajahs knew the secrets for magnetizing valuable works of art and other treasures from all over the world.

MASTERS OF MYSTICAL SECRETS
THAT BROUGHT UNTOLD
WEALTH

In their processions through the streets of the main cities of India their elephants were adorned with scintillating jewels and trappings of gold that dazzled the senses. These fabulous rulers of India were not industrial merchants or stock market investors, they were masters of mystical secrets that had been revealed by the illumined teachers of the past, and simply by sitting in quiet meditation and using the techniques that you are now going to acquire, they projected a stream of psychic energy and magnetized fabulous riches from around the world.

I was fortunate enough to meet one of these great Maharajahs on one of my early visits to India. I was a guest at his magnificent pink palace, and he revealed to me some of the priceless mystical secrets that he had used to build his vast fortune.

THE SECRET POWER OF PSYCHIC
DREAM PROJECTIONS FOR
WEALTH

He told me, "When I was a young man studying at Oxford, I met a Guru from a monastery in Tibet, who was also being educated in London. This illumined Master told me a secret method of psychic dream projection which one could use to attain anything he desired. This method consisted of projecting mental images upon the invisible cosmic protoplasm of the universe of the things that represented money or value. This genetic programming of the higher psychic images duplicated the process in nature in which the cosmic mind we call God stamps upon an orange the duplicate of what is in the genetic structure of the orange seed, or any other seed in nature." By duplicating this mystical process, he claimed, we could project any dream for wealth or other things of value, and the cosmic intelligence would bring about the fulfillment of that psychic dream.

In learning about this mystical process for creating wealth, I remembered the fable about King Midas. This myth actually reflects the mystical process that the Maharajah told me about. Now we shall study this mystical process for turning your dreams into riches and abundance.

STEP-BY-STEP METHOD FOR
USING THE GOLDEN MIDAS
TOUCH

1. Mentally review the fable of the Golden Midas Touch. You will recall that when King Midas did a favor for one of the Gods he was granted any wish that he desired. He asked that everything he touch turn into gold and the wish was granted.

When he touched the furnishings in his palace, they turned into solid gold. He touched the lace tablecloth on his dining table, and it instantly became shimmering gold. Then he put a glass of water to his lips, and the glass and the contents turned to gold. Now trembling, the king took a fork with a piece of meat on it, and they turned into gold! Suddenly, the King became frightened, and when his ten year old daughter ran into the room and threw her arms around her father's neck she turned into a golden statue!

It was then that the king realized his greed had turned the Golden Midas Touch into a Golden Curse and he asked the Gods to remove it.

2. Now, mentally resolve that you will not become greedy, selfish or miserly in your use of the Mystical Golden Touch that you are going to use from now on.

TAKE THE MILLIONAIRE'S
MONEY VOW

Most millionaires have consciously or subconsciously taken a Money Vow in which they made a pact with their higher minds to use their money for the good of the world. Back of every great fortune is this Money Vow:

I vow that I shall use the mystical power of the Golden Midas touch only for good. I shall help members of my family with my newly acquired wealth. I shall do good for humanity. I shall help the poor, the sick, the blind, the handicapped and all others who are unfortunate.

I shall use my money and power to bring peace and brotherhood to the world. I shall try to help others find justice and mercy. I shall be-

queath my treasures to charitable institutions that are capable of doing great good for the human race.

MYSTICAL MONEY VOW BEHIND
THE WORLD'S GREATEST
FORTUNES

In appraising the value of this Money Vow, realize that all the great fortunes of the world have been accumulated by people who have, in turn, helped the world.

The Ford Foundation is doing great good with the money that Henry Ford accumulated.

The Rockefeller Foundation is doing research in medical science that may one day save your life.

The Mellons, who built a vast fortune of millions, endowed one of the greatest art galleries to the world, where thousands of people can see these treasures from all over the world.

J. Paul Getty, who was not known for being overly-generous in his lifetime, left several hundred million dollars to establish museums and art galleries where priceless treasures may be viewed by the public.

Andrew Carnegie who made his vast fortune through steel, gave more than twelve hundred public libraries to the nation that made him rich, and then endowed the cultural institution known as Carnegie Hall for the performing arts. It was in this famous Hall that I gave my lectures on mystical sciences to thousands and thousands of people over the years.

3.   Now, prepare yourself for the Mystical Exercise that will attune your higher psychic mind centers to riches.

Sit quietly in meditation where you will not be disturbed for at least one hour. Say the mystical Mantra AUM, pronounced OHM, five times softly, under your breath. Let the sound of the hum rise into the head area where you will be releasing the spiritual power of the Seventh Chakra, where your psychic third eye is located.

4. Breathe deeply and slowly, holding the breath for only a few seconds and then exhaling it through the mouth. The inhaled breath can be through the nostrils and the exhaled breath expelled through the mouth. Do this ten times, until you feel a deep sense of calmness within your mind and body.

5.   Now, mentally attune your psychic mind centers to money and things of value by thinking these thoughts and saying them quietly to yourself over and over, at least five times each:

I now attune my higher psychic mind centers to money and things of value that I desire.

I mentally project the sum of $1,000 on my mental and psychic screen.

I now see the money in my hands. I count it carefully.

I deposit it in my bank.

I now see myself spending the money and buying things that I desire.

Now you can mentally project larger sums of money on your mental psychic screen. You can say the following:

I now project $5,000 on my psychic screen.

I see the money accumulating in my bank account.

I write checks on this amount for new clothing, a piece of jewelry, a vacation trip to Hawaii.

I now project the sum of $50,000 on my mental psychic screen.

I see a down payment on my dream home. I project opening my own business. I buy a new car and drive it.

6.   You can mentally project sums of money on your mental psychic screen anywhere from $1,000 to $100,000, depending on how much confidence in this power you have built. Do not be afraid to ask for larger sums, for your higher psychic mind centers will respond to your wishes and desires. If you are timid and do not believe in this power to manifest larger sums you will actually paralyze your psychic centers and they cannot respond with creative ideas as to how you shall get these sums of money.

Testimony No. 6

Cyrus D. Projected and Received $50,000

Cyrus D. and his wife Lillian were students in my classes in Psychic Development. They had a desire to manifest wealth. Cyrus worked as a mechanic in a shop and his income was limited to his weekly salary. He was afraid to try something new. Then, when he and his wife learned this method for psychic projection of wealth, they both began to work with the confidence that they would soon have the sum of $50,000.

About this time, the man that Cyrus worked for had a severe heart attack. He made Cyrus the manager while he was recovering from his illness. Cyrus did such a good job and increased the income to such an extent that, when his boss recovered, he made Cyrus an equal partner in the firm. Here was the equivalent of the $50,000 Cyrus and his wife had projected to their higher psychic mind centers! He then set to work in earnest to show his worth, and within one year, his share of the profits was so great that he was able to pay a sizable down payment on a beautiful home and furnish it exactly as they had dreamed of doing.

JOIN THE RANKS OF THE
WEALTHY ARISTOCRACY

7.   You must mentally resolve that you will join the ranks of the wealthy aristocracy by using this mystical secret for building a fortune. When you begin to demonstrate some of the things you have projected to your psychic mind centers, sit quietly in meditation and begin to make specific demands of this higher power within your mind.

Your meditations can be as follows, or you can make up your own powerful statements which you will recite in a low tone:

I give thanks to God for the treasures He has sent me. I now project this psychic stream of riches into outer reality so that I can buy things of tangible value. I mentally project my Dream Home, complete with all the beautiful furnishings I desire. I walk through the rooms of my dream home. I see the furnishings in my living room, beautiful wall-to-wall carpeting on the floors and exquisite drapes at the spacious windows. I entertain friends in my home, serving them on beautiful china in my dining room. My three bedrooms are furnished in good taste, with comfortable beds and beautiful furniture. I project a modern kitchen with all the utilities: a dish washer, a beautiful stove, a modern refrigerator, a deep freezer, fine crystal and china and the best silverware (with two sets of each, one for everyday, the other for special occasions). I now project myself entertaining my friends at a barbecue in my spacious backyard. I see a playground for my children, with a fenced-in yard for their protection.

As you make the above statements you are mentally projecting your innermost dreams to the oversoul of the universe, where your desires are imprinted on a cosmic intelligence that sets to work to materialize these things for you.

Testimony No. 7

Martha A. Projected A Partnership for $100,000

Martha A. worked as a nurse and made good money, but she wanted to increase her income so she and her family could have some of the better things in life.

Martha began to engage herself in periods of psychic meditation, using the techniques given above, projecting the thought that she needed more money to educate her two children, to help her husband with the many burdens of running the house, and to eventually own a home of her own.

One day, while sitting in psychic meditation she had a graphic vision of a beautiful nursing home for wealthy, elderly people. She seemed to be in that home, not as a nurse, but as the proprietor, owning it and running it!

Within a month, she met a retired doctor who wanted to become active again in the medical profession but not work as hard. He told Martha of a beautiful $100,000 estate that he contemplated buying, which he would turn into a nursing home. He asked her if she would like to go into the venture with him and run it in an equal partnership! This was exactly the psychic dream that Martha had had in her meditation sessions. The upshot of this psychic projection was that Martha was soon making more money than she had ever dreamed possible, and at the same time, doing good for suffering humanity. She bought her own home, owned an expensive car, and soon had enough money in the bank to assure her two children of a good education.

COMMAND AND CONTROL THE HIDDEN MYSTICAL FORCES OF THE UNIVERSE TO BRING YOU WEALTH

8. In order to ensure that this mystical method of psychic dream projection will work its miracles for you, begin to practice the secret of your own Psychic Money and Treasure Vault.

As you have learned that the Maharajahs of India used this method to accumulate their fantastic treasures, you can begin to duplicate their magical power through this Treasure Vault secret. You must begin to command and control these hidden mystical forces of the universe to bring you untold wealth. You cannot be lukewarm about it. You must sit down daily and give your imperious commands to this higher spiritual force within your own psychic mind centers.

9.   Stand in front of your mirror and look at the projection of yourself. See that new image as being perfect, in command and control of every life situation. Now say aloud to that Mirror image:

> *I now command and control my mind to project on the psychic*
> *screen of the higher self these mental images:*
> *I desire money to use for constructive purposes.*
> *I desire a business of my own where I can be my own boss.*
> *I desire a true soul mate in love that brings me happiness.*
> *I desire a home of my own where I can rear my family in comfort*
> *and security.*

10.   Now, obtain a box such as is used to put costume jewelry in by ladies or a cuff link box for men. Put a label on this box: MY TREASURE VAULT.

11.   Now, cut out ten pieces of white paper the size and shape of a dollar bill. Put in the four corners the sum of $10,000. The sum total of these pieces of paper is now $100,000.

Each night, before going to bed, count over these pieces of paper which become psychic money equivalents for the sum of $100,000.

When you wish to buy something that costs more money than you now have, count out the exact amount you will need in your Psychic Treasure Vault. If it is $5,000 take out a $10,000 psychic equivalent note, and mentally concentrate on it for five minutes. Say to yourself:

> **I now project the sum of $5,000 from my treasure vault, and I**
> **wish to use it for the following purposes.**

12.   Now mentally review what you want to do with that money. See yourself purchasing what you need, spending it all for the purposes you have projected.

As you need more sums of money, do the same concentration on sums of money from your Treasure Vault. When you have gained tremendous psychic power to project larger and larger sums of money, take ten more pieces of paper, and write $100,000 in each of the four corners. Now the sum total of your psychic money equivalents is $1,000,000. Draw from your Psychic Treasure Vault the sums of money you need. Each night, before going to sleep, concentrate on these larger sums of money, spend them and see yourself having the things that you have mentally projected in your psychic meditations.

13.   You are now ready to place into your Psychic Treasure Vault the various symbols of the things that you wish to project into your life.

Write on a piece of paper; DEED TO MY DREAM HOME. Make out a list of stocks that you wish to own, such as 100 shares of General Electric, 500 shares of General Motors, 100 shares of U.S. Steel, 500 shares of American Telephone and Telegraph. You can obtain the current quotes from your local newspaper, so keep track of your investments, and then mentally see these stocks as belonging to you.

PSYCHIC PORTFOLIO OF RICHES

14.   Now, each night before going to sleep, go into your Psychic Treasure Vault and check over your stocks and your deed to your home. Also, put into this Treasure Vault a small piece of simulated gold, (if you do not have anything of real gold) a piece of silver, a simulated diamond, ruby, emerald and pearl.

15.   Now, when you examine these symbols of wealth each night, give the following meditation:

I now project to my psychic dream self that I shall have these treasures for my very own. I count these treasures and give thanks for them, knowing that my dreams are now being projected to the cosmic mind and being made a glorious reality.

HOW TO ACTIVATE YOUR PSYCHIC PORTFOLIO OF RICHES

16.   When you have placed in your Psychic Portfolio of riches the things that you want to project to the world of reality, it is necessary that you have a ritual in which you activate this higher psychic mind power.

Each night before you go to bed, sit before your treasure vault and go over the stocks, the deed to your dream home, the various sums of simulated money, gold and jewels. Mentally make the following statement to fix these treasures firmly in your higher psychic mind centers:

I an now aware of the treasures of the universe. I transmute these simulated riches for real riches. I enjoy money and the things money can buy. I now project these sums of money, these stocks and

*real estate, these jewels and other treasures to the cosmic mind of
the universe and I ask that they be manifested in my life to give
pleasure to me and my family and to bless the world.*

Testimony No. 8

John N. Projected a Fortune in His Psychic Portfolio

John N. was a gifted musician who played in an Italian restaurant
in Greenwich Village where the waiters sang opera as well as waited on
the customers.

John saw how the place was packed with delighted customers
every night, and the owner was getting rich on his clever idea. John
was originally from a big city in Texas. He used the projection
technique given above. He had placed in his Psychic Portfolio the
various sums of money and the deed to property and his dream home.
He sat in meditation each night, before going to bed, going over his
Psychic Portfolio and asking his higher mind for guidance.

One night, in his dreams, he saw himself opening a similar
restaurant in his home town in Texas. The place was crowded and he
saw himself accompanying the singers and reaping a fortune. When
John awakened he wrote down the vivid dream and then waited to see
what would happen.

In two months time, John found himself back in Texas, he met
someone who backed him in the exact type of restaurant he had
dreamed about, and in that first year of operation, he made $100,000!

MYSTO-MATIC POINTERS

1. *For the next two weeks have a daily money power
   concentration regime of 15 minutes. Concentrate on all
   the treasures in your Treasure Vault and quietly intone
   the money mantra ten times. Ohm-m-o-n-e-y-m-o-n-
   e-y-m-o-n-e-y-m-o-n-e-y-Ohm.*

2. *Go on a psychic windowshopping spree, and claim all
   the beautiful things you see in shop windows as your
   own.*

3. *Stroll through a public park, and claim it as your own with this statement:*

I now claim this park as my private estate to use and enjoy. I here and now take title to it.

4. *For two weeks, every time you spend a $5, $10 or $20 bill, write in the margin: I bless this money. Then affirm to yourself, "I release this money to do good and it shall return to me tenfold."*

5. *Go to a local art gallery and look at all the beautiful art. Get to know the artists, study their lives and enjoy the beauty that they represent. This will enrich your higher consciousness.*

6. *Visit your public library and acquaint yourself with the literature of the past and present. Know the authors' lives, and realize that these treasures belong to you here and now.*

7. *Study the lives of rich people like Rockefeller, Morgan, Vanderbilt, Carnegie, Henry Ford, Edison, Baruch, Andrew Mellon, John Jacob Astor, Hearst, Chrysler and others, to find out their secrets for growing rich.*

3

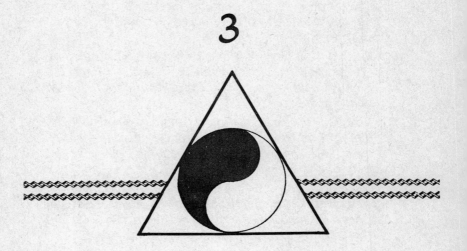

TIBETAN WHITE MAGIC
RITUALS FOR HEALTH,
WEALTH AND LONG LIFE

From beyond the Himalayas, in the ancient land of Tibet, some of the most sacred mysteries have been handed down to modern civilization.

These secrets of Tibetan White Magic can now be used by you to literally perform miracles of healing, accumulating wealth, and achieving a life span of more than one hundred years. Many of these illumined masters in Tibet have been known to live to one hundred and forty years of age. They are masters in the art of psychic transference of thoughts over great distances. They have been known to materialize the astral body at will and project it hundreds of miles, appearing to people in dreams. They have used the forces of White Magic for centuries to rise above the earth realm of problems, sickness, poverty and pain

A BURIED MONASTERY AT THE
FOOT OF THE HIMALAYAS

In recent years, scientists discovered a buried monastery at the foot of the Himalayas where carved wooden plaques were found. These plaques possessed powerful mystic chants, meditations and mantras which have been forbidden secrets through the ages.

I have been fortunate enough to obtain literal translations of these ancient plaques and now present for your use these mystical rituals that will release the Tibetan White Magic forces in your own life.

In the sacred book of Tibet known as the *Song Celestial,* you will find these rituals of white magic that can literally transform your life into transcendental beauty, peace, love and happiness.

Let us now explore these forbidden secrets of the ages and learn how to release the White Magic Tibetan power to overcome the negative forces of life.

HOW TO FOCUS PSYCHO-ASTRAL
RAYS ON YOUR PSYCHIC SCREEN

1.   Before you can release the Psycho-Astral Rays that can bring you anything in life that you desire, it is necessary that you clear your mind of all the negative forces that are known as Black Magic, so you can focus the pure light of Infinite Intelligence on the psychic screen of your higher mind.

The ancient Tibetans used the majestic Himalaya mountains as focal points of concentration, in an exercise which they called Ascension to the Spiritual Mountain Top. As they mentally ascended this symbolical mountain, they gradually rose above the mortal mind's realm of problems, worries, sickness, fear, hate, discord, poverty and limitation. To achieve this ascension to the spiritual mountain top, sit quietly where you will not be disturbed for at least half an hour. Close your eyes and go into meditation as follows:

Relax your mind and body by gently humming the sacred mantra AUM, pronounced OHM, about ten times. Breathe deeply each time you exhale the breath on the AUM, and gradually slow down the frequency of your breathing.

2.   Now, mentally visualize the sacred mountain peak, with your eyes closed. See the spiritual mountain top rising high above the troubled earthly plane. See the rosy clouds surrounding the peak of the mountain. Then, mental-

ly project yourself to that mountain top with the following mystic meditation statement:

> *I now rise to the spiritual mountain top. I rise above the limited earthly plane of problems and limitations. I am now pure spirit liberated from the world of pain, sickness, war and death. I now project my soul into the peaceful realm of Shangri-La where I am in the eternal springtime of my soul's immortality. All the dark shadows of earth now drop away from me. I now clear my mind of all the negative forces of the earth and my soul is bathed in the white magic Astral rays of peace, harmony, happiness, joy and love.*

3.   You can hold this meditation for a period of five to ten minutes, giving yourself a chance to clear all the built-up tensions and anxieties from your higher consciousness. Visualize your mind being like a clear cut prism, through which is reflected a white beam of light. As a prism splits up a white beam of light into all the astral colors of the rainbow, you will now visualize these Psycho-Astral Rays as cerulean blue, for peace; golden sunlight yellow, for happiness; viridian green for health and healing, if you should be sick; rosy sunrise pink for love happiness; pale orchid or lilac for soul serenity; vibrant red-orange for youthful vitality and energy; and ultra-marine blue for business success, riches and abundance.

4.   You are now ready to project the white magic of Psycho-Astral Rays to achieve these various elements that you desire in your life. But first, you must understand the difference between white magic and black magic.

As black is the absence of white, it represents the negative polarity in the seven astral rays of the rainbow. White includes all the seven colors of the rainbow, and when you use the white magic forces, you automatically cancel out all the evil forces of black magic. In the Tantric Mysticism from ancient Tibet it is recognized that both negative and positive forces do exist in the universe. The Tibetan mystic does not try to get rid of evil, for this is impossible; he simply substitutes good for evil and the evil disappears.

Just as shadows are unreal and can be dispelled when you turn on the light, black magic forces are removed when you become illumined with these Psycho-Astral Rays of good, peace, beauty, joy, charity and divine love.

5.   You must now learn these two opposing polarities that exist in the universe so you may transmute the negative forces of black magic into the positive forces of white magic.

NEGATIVE FORCES	POSITIVE FORCES
EVIL (Devil)	GOOD (God)
DISEASE	HEALTH
MISERY	HAPPINESS
POVERTY	RICHES
DISCORD	PEACE
HATE	LOVE
FAILURE	SUCCESS
UGLINESS	BEAUTY
DEATH	ETERNAL LIFE

6.   Now you are ready to project the Psycho-Astral Rays of white magic to dispel the above negative forces of black magic. Remember, do not try to change people or conditions! As a mystic you must work in the higher realm of spirit to overcome these negative forces that are called "The Earth Hinderances."

As you now sit in meditation, repeat the scared AUM ten times, slow down the breathing gradually and relax your mind and body. Keep your eyes closed as you do these white magic rituals. At first you may have to keep them open to read these instructions, but later, as you acquire proficiency in this mystical art, you can keep your eyes closed, as it helps in achieving better concentration.

WHITE MAGIC RITUAL AND MEDITATION FOR PEACE OF MIND

I now concentrate my mind on the Psycho-Astral Ray of cerulean blue for peace of mind and inner tranquility. I attune my mind to the sweet harmony of the music of the spheres. My mind is like a peaceful lake reflecting the blue skies and the golden sun. There are no ripples on the surface of the mental lake and I dwell in peace and harmony with those around me. As light banishes darkness, I now become illumined by the sacred, golden presence of God or good, and I banish all evil forces from my consciousness and from my environment.

Testimony No. 9

How Wilma K. Overcame Discord and Unhappiness in Marriage

Wilma K. was a lecture member who learned about these Psycho-Astral Rays of white magic. She had been miserable for many months because of the lack of love response on the part of her husband. She also had in-law trouble, as her husband's mother made her home with them. There was constant friction and discord. She was sick half the time and unable to concentrate on doing her housework. She felt so miserable at times that she contemplated suicide, but the thought of her two children being left behind kept her from taking this drastic step to end her misery.

After she told me her tragic story, I knew that she would have to work hard to overcome the projection of the mother-in-law's black magic forces, as it was obvious they hated each other.

I gave Wilma the White Magic ritual given in section 2 of this chapter, for clearing her mind of the negative, black magic forces. She was able to do this twice a day until she began to feel free of the debilitating effects of the negative pull towards destruction and disaster.

Then, I fashioned a special meditation ritual for Wilma, which anyone may use who has a similar problem of discord and friction in the home with their marriage partners. The following meditation ritual was to be repeated twice a day until the negative forces were completely dispelled:

> *I am now surrounded by the white magic aura of happiness, success, health and romance. I attune my soul to the soul rhythm of the universe. I become loving and forgiving, gentle and kind. I see my husband as the other half of a magic circle of love. I now unite my mind, body and soul with his, in a perpetual song of harmony, peace, beauty, joy, good and love. I unite with the magic circle of God's infinite love and beauty and I am healed of all discordant thoughts and unpleasant emotions. I forgive my mother-in-law and bless her. I surround her with the white magic light of infinite peace and love. My life is serene. My romance is restored. I am happy in all departments of my life.*

Within two weeks, Wilma reported to me that the situation was changing; she felt more peaceful and relaxed. Her mother-in-law seemed to actually be making efforts at understanding her better and treating her like a human being. Best of all, her husband began to show more love than usual, giving her assurances that he would be different in the future.

WHITE MAGIC RITUAL AND
MEDITATION FOR HAPPINESS

7. Sit quietly in meditation and project the Psycho-Astral Ray of golden sunlight yellow. Visualize this ray as cascading from the celestial heights like the sun's life-giving rays. Say the sacred AUM ten times, breathe slowly and deeply and think or say the following White Magic meditation ritual:

> *I now concentrate my mind on the Psycho-Astral Ray of golden sunlight for achieving a state of perpetual happiness. I realize that the shadows of fear, hostility, worry, hate, doubt and anxiety that cloud the horizons of my mind are unreal. I now dispel these shadows with the golden light of truth. I ascend the spiritual mountaintop where I can look into the unlimited vistas of God's eternality, and my soul blends with the soul of the universe in a triumphal rainbow of golden dreams.*

Testimony No. 10

How Fred T. Overcame Depression

Fred T. suffered from chronic moodiness and depression. Everything, including shock therapy and drugs, had been tried, but to no avail. Fred feared losing his job, which he had done several times before. This threw him into deeper states of melancholy. Finally, his wife was unable to stand being with him, and she deserted him. It was then that Fred sought out spiritual help in our work at Carnegie Hall.

I gave Fred the mind-clearing meditation in section 2 of this chapter and the meditation given above. He kept up this projection of the Psycho-Astral Rays for happiness, adding to it the ritual given for peace of mind and inner tranquility. Results were almost immediate. Fred was able to break the black magic curse of misery and discontent and soon began to see that life was worth living and that it could be beautiful.

In three weeks' time Fred had won back his wife's love and they were building a new life together, like a young romantic couple!

WHITE MAGIC RITUAL AND
MEDITATION FOR HEALING

8.   You can use these Psycho-Astral Rays for healing your body if you should become sick and also for keeping your body healthy, vital and energetic to a ripe old age.

To achieve a healing of any physical condition, you must first have faith in this higher, spiritual power. It is the God-mind that created you and it is this same mind, working through your higher psychic mind centers that sustains you daily, nourishes your body, causes your heart to beat, your blood to circulate, and the defense mechanism of your body to kill invading germs and keep you healthy.

Testimony No. 11

Rita R. Suffered Chronic Illness Before Seeking Help

Rita R. suffered chronically from colds, bronchial asthma, painful sinus infections and other ailments of the respiratory tract. She had tried every known form of therapy and drugs and nothing seemed to relieve her. She was unhappy in her work and her husband had left her and her two children for another woman. Her co-workers found her cross and irritable. Doctors tried injecting her with fifty different substances they thought she might be allergic to, but nothing seemed to work. It was in this state of desperation that Rita turned to our work in Spiritual Healing for help.

Following is the regimen given to Rita R. for achieving a healing of her condition. You can use this same method for releasing Psycho-Astral Rays of healing to any part of your body that you wish to heal.

Sit in meditation and repeat the sacred mantra AUM ten times. Relax the mind and body completely. With the eyes closed, visualize a golden ball of light in the head area. You are now going to direct this ball of light to the part of the body which is afflicted. You can visualize this golden ball of light traveling to that area of the body, while you repeat the following healing meditation. You can read this healing statement at first, until you either memorize it or learn to make up your own.

*I now direct the golden light of healing to my entire head area to
help me overcome my sinus condition and then I direct it to the
lungs and chest area, to heal my bronchial and respiratory condition. This golden light of healing carries with it the Psycho-Astral
Rays of the sun and all other planets, with their magnetism,
electricity and other invisible elements. I now direct this healing
force to give me complete healing of this condition.*

Testimony No. 12

Murray B. Kept His Heart Vital with Psycho-Astral Rays

Another case where Psycho-Astral Rays were used for achieving
a miracle healing was that of Murray B. who had suffered two severe
heart attacks that were nearly fatal. He could no longer go to work, his
activities were strictly curtailed and he was convinced that he would
soon have another heart attack that would kill him. It was at this time
that his wife urged him to seek out this form of spiritual therapy to help
heal his heart condition.

In Murray's case, he was told to direct the Psycho-Astral healing
ray to his heart, with the following direct commands:

*I now direct the healing rays to my heart. As the golden light of
God's healing power flows through my bloodstream, propelled by
my beating heart, it is doing the work of healing every atom and cell
of my brain and body.*
*I direct the cosmic life energy to flow through my heart. I know that
the heart is one of the strongest muscles in my body, intended to
pump the life energy for one hundred years or more. I now feel its
healing rays giving my heart new life and energy. It now beats in
rhythm to the cosmic life force at seventy-two beats a minute. I am
healed, I am healed, I am healed.*

HEALING OF OTHER PARTS OF
THE BODY THROUGH
PSYCHO-ASTRAL RAYS

Just as you have learned to direct the Psycho-Astral healing rays to the
head area and the heart, you can also direct these healing rays to the stomach,
gall bladder, reproductive organs, kidneys, colon, liver and spleen. If there is
congestion or inflammation in any of these areas, you can sit in meditation,

bathe yourself mentally in the viridian green healing Astral ray, and then direct the golden ball of light to that part of the body that is afflicted.

GALL BLADDER INFLAMMATION
AND TUMORS OVERCOME
THROUGH PSYCHO-ASTRAL RAYS

I have seen cases of severe gall bladder inflammation completely overcome in a period of two weeks by daily treatment of fifteen minutes, twice a day.

I have personally known of cases of swollen tumors that were caused to dissolve and disappear through this type of projection of the Psycho-Astral healing rays, in a period of from one to three months, depending on the size of the tumors.

WHITE MAGIC RITUAL AND
MEDITATION FOR LOVE
HAPPINESS

9.   These Psycho-Astral Rays may be used to heal other negative conditions besides sickness. They can be projected to the higher psychic mind centers to overcome romantic and marital problems.

If you have difficulties in your love life or marriage, sit in quiet meditation at least fifteen minutes a day and see the Psycho-Astral Ray of rosy, sunrise pink surrounding you. Then do the sacred AUM ten times, and relax as you breathe deeply and slowly, saying the following meditation statement to yourself:

> *I now attune my higher mind centers to the Psycho-Astral Ray of divine love. I know that God intended for me to find my true soul mate and I now project the love magnetism that will attract my perfect mate to me. I ask for intuitive guidance for finding my soul mate. I know that God is love and I am now attuned to the higher cosmic wavelengths of spiritual and physical love.*

Testimony No. 13

Pearl H. Finds Her Future Husband and Business Partner

One of my lecture members, Pearl H., had been disappointed in love and marriage twice. She was bitter and disillusioned when she came into our work, but learned how to use advanced laws of Mysticism for finding true love fulfillment. She had a desire to attract her true soul mate, to own a beautiful home, and to go into a business which she could run with her future husband.

She fixed all these three desires in her Blueprint of Destiny, and then gave herself the following Psycho-Astral Ray projection to achieve all three objectives:

I now project the dream I have for my true soul mate. I wish to attract a man who is loving, kind and spiritual. I project a dream home which we shall share together. I wish to go into some business where we can work together and find financial security. I ask for divine guidance as to the fulfillment of these dreams and desires.

Each day for fifteen minutes, twice a day, Pearl used the above white magic projections, and without making any effort on her part, she was directed by her intuitive, psychic mind, to attend a dance being given by her church. She was then introduced to a man who had recently come to town. They danced together and for Pearl it was love at first sight.

After that night, they saw each other several times and Pearl knew intuitively that this was the man of her dreams. Sure enough, on their fourth date together, he told her he loved her and asked her to marry him. After their honeymoon, they settled down together in the perfect dream home she had visualized. It just so happened that her husband was in real estate and had just transferred his interests to her town. She was asked to go into the business with him, and every single facet of her mental projection was fulfilled.

WHITE MAGIC RITUAL FOR SOUL SERENITY

10.   When you are mentally disturbed and your life seems to be filled with problems that are unsolvable, you can use the Psycho-Astral Ray of orchid or lilac as your meditation color and give yourself the following white magic treatment to help restore balance, harmony and soul serenity:

My soul is now attuned to the soul of the universe. I grow wings of the spirit and soar above the limited earth plane with its problems, tragedies and misfortunes. I sing the Song Celestial, and my soul vibrates to the joyous wavelengths of peace, infinite good, radiant beauty, eternal love and spiritual fulfillment. My soul blends with the soul of the universe in the magic circle of God's divine love and I know the soul's peace and serenity for all time.

WHITE MAGIC RITUAL FOR
BUSINESS SUCCESS, RICHES AND
ABUNDANCE

11.   As you sit in meditation to project the Psycho-Astral Rays for achieving business success, riches and abundance, mentally bathe your aura with the astral color of ultra-marine blue.

Repeat the sacred AUM ten times, breathe deeply, and think or say the following meditation:

> *I now project the Psycho-Astral Ray of success in every department of my life. I attune my higher psychic mind to the cosmic mind and I receive brilliant ideas that can make me successful in every way. I ask for guidance for going into my right life work. I attune my mind to the concept of universal riches, so I shall attract a constant flow of riches to meet my every need. I know that I have inherited the universe and all therein. I now accept my divine inheritance of riches and abundance and give thanks for all my present and future blessings.*

MYSTO-MATIC POINTERS

1.   *Give yourself a special Psycho-Astral Ray treatment for each day of the week.*

> *Monday:*   *Today I live in the awareness of my white magic forces of happiness, health, peace, good and love.*
>
> *Tuesday:*   *I am aware of the new self-image I have created and project confidence, poise and inner power to the outer world.*
>
> *Wednesday:*   *Today I shall use my Golden Magic Touch and obtain something of value from every person I meet.*
>
> *Thursday:*   *All day today I am in God's magic circle of golden light that makes me immune to life's problems.*
>
> *Friday:*   *Today I claim the parks as my estates, the libraries and art galleries as my sources of inspiration. I am rich in consciousness.*

Saturday: *I radiate divine love to every person I meet.*

Sunday: *I am aware of God's presence in His Creation and I give thanks for the gift of life.*

2. Avoid using black magic statements such as, "I am poor. I am unhappy. I was born to lose. I am lonely and unloved."

3. Use white magic statements, "I have inherited the universe. I am happy. I was born to win. I am beloved and joyous. I am rich.

4. Sit in the stillness and visualize your mind like a peaceful still lake, without a ripple on the surface. Try to maintain that stillness.

5. Sit in daily meditation and ask your higher psychic mind for guidance as to what you should do each day of your life.

4

OPEN WIDE YOUR PSYCHIC THIRD EYE: SEE INTO THE INVISIBLE WORLD OF PSYCHIC PHENOMENA

There are many forms of psychic phenomena which you may use to shape your future destiny. In mysticism, the ancients in India, Tibet, China and Egypt taught that every person possesses the power of prophecy and that everyone can develop the psychic third eye to have constant intuitive guidance in every situation of life.

In this chapter, you will be shown how to develop and use this natural psychic gift to avoid life's misfortunes and tragedies. You can receive daily guidance from your higher psychic mind centers so that you will do the right thing at the right time.

You can train this higher psychic mind to reveal for you the hidden secrets behind life. You can begin to read people and know their secret, innermost thoughts and motivations. You can know your future, because this higher psychic mind gives you a preview of that future and then automatically guides you to its complete fulfillment.

For example, you may sit in psychic reverie and have the intuitive guidance to take a certain form of action, without knowing consciously why you are doing it. As a result of that action you will be guided to fullfilling some aspect of your future destiny. This is indirectly the result of your psychic guidance.

Testimony No. 14

Jennie L. Attracted Her Soul Mate Through Psychic Power

Jennie L. was a student in mysticism in our Carnegie Hall classes some years ago. She worked as a secretary and yet she did not feel completely satisfied doing that work. She felt she would be happy as an artist. As she had developed her psychic third eye, she projected this dream and also the romantic vision that she would meet her ideal soul mate and find happiness in marriage.

One day while coming to Carnegie Hall, Jennie passed by the Art Students League, which is a short distance away. She stopped to look at the students' work in the windows, and some compelling urge caused her to go in and inquire about taking an evening course in painting and drawing.

As she was motivated by her psychic mind, Jennie could not know the real reason for attending these classes in art, but her higher mind knew the hidden mosaic of her life and impelled her to study art. Jennie, by her own admission, never felt she would be a great artist, but she enrolled in the classes and enjoyed this hobby.

It so happened that one of the instructors at the Art Students League was a good-looking young man who had been assigned to Jennie's class. Within a short time, he began to show an unusual interest in Jennie's work, and they were soon dating. They had so much in common that Jennie found herself falling in love with him, and the young man responded immediately.

Now, the hidden pattern of destiny began to reveal itself to Jennie. Her psychic mind centers had known, in some mysterious fashion, that she would find fulfillment in love and marriage through her desire to study art! She was motivated to enroll in the art classes so she could meet her perfect soul mate. Later, after they had married, Jennie introduced the young man to me, and I explained to her how she had been really guided by her psychic centers to meeting her future husband. As this event could have occurred in dozens of different ways, it remained for her higher psychic mind to choose the one path that would lead Jennie to the finding of her soul mate, which happened to be through a study of art.

REMOVE NEGATIVE CLOUDBANKS TO HAVE PERFECT PSYCHIC VISION

Your higher psychic mind centers will create the perfect destiny for you if you do not let the cloudbanks of negativity interfere with the flow of power from the Cosmic Mind of God. Before you begin to develop your own higher psychic powers, sit in a meditation session of about half an hour or so, do the following mental exercise to remove the cloudbanks of fear, worry, hate, greed, selfishness and animalism from your psychic mind centers.

Repeat this dynamic psychic clearing meditation, reading it to yourself several times. Do this every day until you find that your psychic centers are no longer clouded and they begin to function perfectly:

I now direct my higher mind to rid my psychic centers of all negative thoughts of every kind. I overcome fear and worry by supplanting them with faith and confidence that a higher spiritual power can guide and protect me. I remove hate and supplant it with the divine emotion of love. I overcome tendencies to greed, selfishness and animalism by attuning my higher mind to the God mind in the universe. I am yoked to God's cosmic intelligence, and He guides me every day of my life.

HOW TO OPEN THE MYSTIC THIRD EYE FOR PSYCHIC VISION

When your psychic centers are cleared of these cloudbanks of negative emotions, you are ready to sit in daily development sessions for achieving psychic phenomena. Sit quietly in meditation, where you will not be disturbed for at least one hour, and follow these instructions. Close your physical eyes as you do these psychic exercises:

1. Direct your concentration to the forefront of your brain, where the psychic third eye is located. Try to visualize this as an actual eye that has the power of inner vision.

2. Now close your physical eyes and breathe deeply to the count of four. Hold the breath to the count of four and then release it.

3. Your inhaled breath is the pranic life force, called Celestial Fire by the mystics of the far east. It is this stream of pranic life energy that flows to your psychic centers, opening the third eye and causing it to have psychic vision. Do this breathing about five times, holding the breath each time to the count of four before you release it.

4. Now, to open this psychic center, visualize a small screen inside your forehead, very much like your TV screen. For practice sessions you will now learn how to read your psychic projections on this mental, psychic screen.

5. Now you will ask this higher psychic mind for clairvoyant vision to prophesy the events of your future.

6. Consciously project some definite picture forms on this psychic screen, such as your future dream home. You can mentally write on your mental screen the words, "MY DREAM HOME." Flash that sentence onto the psychic screen just as though you were watching a neon light flashing a message on a visible sign. You can make the color gold, blue, pink, white or any color you choose.

7. You can now ask this question of your psychic mind: "Show me a picture of my future dream home and guide me to finding the perfect home that I desire."

8. As you sit in the silence, with your eyes closed, concentrate all your thoughts onto that psychic screen within your own mind. As you hold your thoughts on your dream home you will begin to get flashes

of pictures of homes that you may have seen in the past. As your psychic mind centers are imprinted by your own secret dreams and desires, it is natural that you will find projected on your psychic screen the exact prototype of the home you wish to live in.

Testimony No. 15

Psychic Power Helped Mr. and Mrs. T.R. Find Their Dream Home

An example of how this psychic mind works to direct us to the fulfillment of destiny is that of a couple I once knew who studied these laws of psychic phenomena with me in classes. Mr. and Mrs. T.R. had been married for two years and already had one child, so they wanted to move into larger quarters.

They sat in daily psychic development sessions using the above method of psychic projection for their "Dream Home." They both had the same vision of a home with three bedrooms, a large yard for children, located near a school. They pictured it already furnished, as they had money for a downpayment but not enough to completely furnish such a home.

One night they attended a church social where they were introduced to a middle-aged couple. The husband was a retired doctor, and they mentioned during the course of conversation that their three children were married and they wanted to sell their home and move to Ft. Lauderdale in Florida, where one of their children lived with his growing family.

Instantly, Mr. and Mrs. T.R. were interested and felt that in some mysterious way they were being guided to the fulfillment of their psychic vision for their perfect Dream Home.

They made an appointment to look at the house and, to their delight, it was exactly as they had projected their vision of their dream home! It was even furnished in modern furniture and the yard had a fence around it, as they had also projected. The wonderful thing about this entire psychic revelation was that the doctor and his wife had plenty of money, they owned the home outright and did not require a huge downpayment. Mr. and Mrs. T.R. were able to move in right after escrow was closed and their psychic dream was fulfilled perfectly!

HOW TO OBTAIN LARGE SUMS OF MONEY THROUGH PSYCHIC GUIDANCE

1.   You can also use psychic phenomena to guide you in obtaining large sums of money to meet your future requirements and pay your present bills.

When you go into Psychic Reverie, which is called daydreaming by some, hold the sum of money that you wish to attract in your mind's eye. This can be $1,000 for current needs or it may be $5,000 or $10,000 that you require for the year's extra expenses or for purchasing a car, or household furnishings. You can also project a larger sum such as $100,000 or $500,000 or even $1,000,000 for future financial security. Here is how you project any of these amounts to your higher psychic mind centers.

2.   You can start out asking your psychic mind for smaller sums of money, like $100 or $500 so as to build your faith in larger sums gradually. Sit with your eyes closed, do the breathing and mental projection of your psychic screen, but now instead of seeing houses or cars or other objects, mentally project the sum of money onto the screen. See the $100 or $500 in a flashing neon light. Keep flashing this psychic sign for at least five minutes, or until it is fixed firmly in your consciousness.

3.   Then you can open your eyes and read the following directions to your psychic mind centers:

I ask for the sum of $100 to manifest in my life in the next few days. I need this sum of money for immediate expenses. Guide me to this money to meet my present needs.

If it is $500 or $1,000 you require, use the same statement as above, but substitute the figure of $500 or $1,000.

Testimony No. 16

Rosita E. Attracted an Expensive Color T.V. Set

After you have given these instructions to your higher psychic mind go about your ordinary activities, confident that the money will come. It may come as equivalents rather than cash. One woman, Rosita E. asked her higher mind for $500 so she could buy a color TV set. The money did not come, but her next door neighbor was moving from New York to Kentucky. She had a large color TV set that she did not want to move, so she offered it to this woman for only $100. It was in perfect condition and one of the expensive models that cost about $800. Therefore, Rosita actually received more than the $500 she was asking for.

FIND LOST OBJECTS WITH
PSYCHIC POWER

1. Your higher psychic mind can often reveal the location of lost or hidden objects. If you lose a valuable piece of jewelry, sit in meditation, and project to this higher mind: "Show me where my ring is." Sit in the stillness for a few moments, repeating the question, and then quietly go about your everyday activities. Generally, within a short time you will automatically be guided to where the lost object is.

Testimony No. 17

Sybil S. Was Guided to Finding Her Lost Ring

Sybil S. had taken off her engagement ring and mislaid it. She was frantic, not because of the value of the diamond, but because of the sentiment attached to the ring. She searched everywhere frantically and could not find it. Then she remembered that in a class on psychic development I had said to go into psychic reverie and ask where the lost object was, and then to relax and go about one's usual activities.

Sybil did this and a short time later as she was about to empty a bag of trash that was near the sink in the kitchen. She suddenly saw a bright object glisten in the bag and looked inside. There she found her diamond ring! She had removed it, set it on the kitchen sink just above the paper bag, and it had been nudged into the bag. As she was now sensitively attuned to her higher psychic mind, it chose this method for revealing the lost object.

2.   To find hidden treasures, gold, oil, water or other things in the soil, there is a method called dousing which has been used with great success by many people. They use a dousing rod, which begins to tremble when it is over a location of something valuable. Your higher psychic mind can be attuned like a dousing rod, so before you go in search of treasures or hidden springs of water, you can sit in the stillness and say to this psychic mind: "I wish to locate valuables in the earth. Guide me to the location of these hidden treasures."

Testimony No. 18.

Fred J. Was Guided to an Abandoned Mine
Through Psychic Power

Fred J. went out to an old abandoned gold mine in Nevada, having studied psychic development in our classes. He walked over the area where the mine had been worked years before and asked the question: "Is there more gold hidden here?" He got such a positive feeling that he entered the old mine and began to dig in a certain location. He finally broke through a thin wall and discovered a vein of gold that eventually brought him more than $35,000. If he had not sensitively attuned his mind to the finding of this treasure he would never have been led by his psychic mind to that particular gold mine.

3.   After you begin to ask your psychic mind for sums of money begin to keep books on the various things that come to you which might be equivalents of money, such as gifts, theater tickets, clothing, furniture and other things of value.

Testimony No. 19

Bernice E. Projected a Valuable Mink Coat

Bernice E. lived in New York where winters can be very severe. She projected she wanted $1,000 to buy a fur coat. Within two weeks her psychic mind centers brought her in contact with a wealthy woman, for whom Bernice occasionally did catering work when she entertained at home. It was a miserable, snowy night, and as Bernice was about to put on her shabby cloth coat, the woman remarked, "Why, that coat won't keep you warm in such a storm." She paused a moment and then said, "Wait a moment." She went into her bedroom and returned with a beautiful black mink coat that must have cost several thousands dollars. She said to Bernice, "My husband just gave me a brand new mink coat and I want you to have this one as I have no further use for it."

4.   The art of precognition, or knowing the future, can be developed as a psychic gift. You can sit in psychic reverie and ask that your higher mind reveal certain events in your future. These events may come as pictures shown on your mental screen, or you may have a prophetic dream in which you will see yourself acting out your life story in the future.

Testimony No. 20

Leila O. Warned of an Airplane Crash

Leila O. had a strange psychic dream which she could not understand at the time. She saw a bright red airplane circling in the sky against a brilliant blue background. Suddenly the engine stopped and the plane began to fall to earth. At that moment she glanced at the clock on the airport tower and it said two o'clock. She awakened from the dream and was puzzled as to its meaning. A few weeks later she took her friend Dorothy to the airport for a flight to Chicago. As they stood waiting to board the plane, they heard the sound of a plane engine that was plainly in distress. Leila looked up and there was a bright red plane against a cerulean blue sky, falling to earth! It crashed, killing the pilot and his passenger. Leila had been given a psychic premonition of that event through her prophetic dream weeks before.

5.   When you ask your higher psychic mind for guidance or revelations for your future, do not expect an answer immediately. As your conscious mind is constantly intruding its own opinions for your evaluation, you must wait until such time as your conscious mind is still or is occupied with other matters. It is then that your psychic mind will often send you the answers to your questions or the solutions to your problems.

Make it a point to sit for a few moments in psychic reverie, ask your questions and then quietly go about your everyday activities. Suddenly, you will be compelled to do certain things that could lead you to the finding of the solution to a problem or the answer to some baffling question.

USE PSYCHIC REVERIE FOR
AUTOMATIC CREATIVE GIFTS
AND TALENTS

1.   You can achieve automatic writing, speaking or painting, by sitting in psychic reverie and asking for the particular gift you wish to develop. Say to this higher mind: "I wish to become an artist (or a writer, inventor, composer or speaker)" and then you can add: "Show me how to develop my gifts in this direction."

You will find yourself being guided to the course of study you need or a person who will inspire you to develop the gift or talent that you possess. Your higher psychic mind knows if you have the ability to do the creative work you ask for, and if you do not have, you will find that there is no response from this higher mind center.

HOW TO USE CLAIRAUDIENCE TO
HEAR PSYCHIC MESSAGES

2.   Clairaudience means to hear with an inner ear when the voice of the spirit speaks to you. Many times, people have actually heard a guiding voice, like Joan of Arc did when she had her psychic revelation that she was to lead the armies of France to victory. Sometimes the voice comes in an intuitive way,

speaking to your higher mind as an impulse to do a certain thing at a certain time. This then becomes the voice of the spirit, and it often speaks to you naturally, through your imagination or through your own conscious mind when you are in stillness.

3.   If you wish this higher psychic power to manifest through you in automatic writing, sit in stillness with a pen and paper before you. Ask this higher mind to give you some specific information, such as an article for publication, or the beginning of a story or novel. Do not try to force the pen to write, but try to attune your mind to the higher psychic mind, so you can receive its divine inspiration when it comes through. If you do this daily you will soon acquire a sensitivity to its promptings and you will begin to write without effort. Most great authors receive their communications from this higher cosmic mind that works through their own psychic mind centers. This art is difficult to develop but it can be done. You can also use it for automatic speaking and for painting or other art work.

ASK QUESTIONS OF YOUR
PSYCHIC MIND AND RECEIVE
RIGHT ANSWERS

4.   Another way by which you can develop your higher psychic mind centers is by sitting in quiet meditation and simply asking your higher mind to guide you. You can write down questions like this and then take them into your developing sessions and ask that they be answered by your psychic mind:

- Can I trust this person in a business venture?
- Should I quit my job and seek another one?
- Where should I move . . to California, Florida or stay where I am?
- How can I meet my true soul mate?
- Should I buy this house at this time?
- Is it safe to take this trip?
- Is my mate being true to me?
- Should I go into my own business and what kind?
- How can I solve this problem in my life?

Many times when you submit questions to the higher psychic mind, the answer does not come during your waking hours. It may come as a vision while you sleep. These clairvoyant dreams are often symbolic and can point out things you need to know.

Testimony No. 21

Richard W. Was Guided to the Right Stock Through a Dream

Richard W. was a small investor in the stock market. He asked the question. "Should I invest in the stock market now?" A few nights later, he had a vivid dream in which he saw a white eagle soaring against a bright blue sky. He awakened from his dream and then recalled that in one of my classes on mysticism I had mentioned that the sign of Scorpio had two symbols, one was that of a stinging scorpion, the other was that of an eagle. He happened to be a Scorpio and this dream seemed to be trying to tell him something, he later told me.

The following day, while going over a list of stocks, he noticed one called White Eagle, which was at an all time low of about one dollar a share. On blind faith he bought five thousand shares of the stock and held it for some time. The stock finally went to seven dollars a share and Richard sold it, making a very nice profit.

Testimony No. 22

Sandra V. Found a $15,000 Bonanza

Another instance in which a clairvoyant dream came to a woman who desperately needed money, was that of Sandra V., whose mother had died. There were heavy funeral expenses, and as Sandra's father had died some years before and she was alone, she asked her higher psychic mind how she could obtain money to meet all her bills and give her security until she could get a job. A few nights later, she had a vivid dream in which her mother came to her, just as she had been in life and said, "I know you are terribly worried because there is no money but I have saved quite a little and you will find it in that old dresser that is stored in the basement." When Sandra awakened, it seemed she could still hear her mother's voice ringing in her ears. She went to the old dresser and searched it. There, in a hidden compartment she found a big wad of old bills that totalled $15,000:

Many times, the souls of those who have departed are able to relay a message to those of us left on earth. If we have become sensitively attuned to this cosmic spirit behind the universe, this type of telepathetic communication between the departed loved ones and those on earth becomes possible.

MYSTO-MATIC POINTERS

1. *You are more closely attuned to people who are emotionally close to you like your mother or father, your husband or wife. You can tune in on them psychically through mental telepathy when you wish to receive important information about them.*

2. *When trying to reach a person psychically, hold the face of the person in your mind or look at a picture of that person and then talk to them just as if they were there in person.*

3. *Do not try to receive psychic messages when mentally disturbed. Sit quietly until your mind is calm and then project your thoughts.*

4. *Sometimes, the answer to one of your questions will come through while you are busy doing something else; it will seem like your own mind speaking, so be aware of this and listen to that still, small voice.*

5. *Clairvoyance and clairaudience can often come to you through your dreams, so jot down any unusual dreams.*

6. *A message will often come to you through a book or by running your finger down the bible; you will be caused to stop on the line that fits your needs.*

7. *Psychic guidance may sometimes come to you through imagination. A flash of a picture or a name or a sentence will be revealed by your higher psychic mind through your imagination.*

8. Distance is no barrier to sending psychic messages. You can reach people who are thousands of miles distant by persistently calling the name and sending your message.

9. Look for answers to your needs through psychic dreams or visions that may come while sitting in meditation.

5

HOW MYSTIC CHANTS, MEDITATIONS AND MANTRAS SPARK MIRACLE AFTER MIRACLE

There is something within every human being that makes him long for a mystical experience. His soul has an intense, pulsating desire to communicate with a higher spiritual power, which Emerson called "The soul of the Universe."

It is natural for you to search in the unseen, invisible realm for a living Spiritual Reality which created you and which sustains you throughout your earthly life experience.

In this chapter you will learn how to use the three forms of mysticism which can cause you to ascend the spiritual mountaintop, where you can see into eternity. There, the answer to any problem will appear as if by magic.

The Mystics of ancient Tibet, India and China, taught that this pathway to heaven could only be reached through the inner self. By going into quiet meditation and reciting certain mystical chants and mantras the searcher of truth could attune his mind and soul to the invisible pulsations of the universal spirit, which man has named God. There is a subtle pulsation or celestial rhythm in the universe, which the ancients called "the music of the spheres."

THE MYSTIC KEY OF MEDITATION TO SECRETS OF THE UNIVERSE

There is a mystic key to the secrets of the universe. This is the power of meditation, in which you can attune your mind and soul to the rhythm of the universe. When your mind and spirit are thus attuned to the universal rhythm, tremendous power is released in your higher psychic mind centers. You can then motivate people, you can demand sums of money from life and they will come, you can decree that the world give you recognition, fame and fortune and it cannot be denied you. You can tune in on the magnetic wavelength of love and people will be irresistably drawn to you like a magnet.

HOW TO ACHIEVE THE FIRST STAGE OF MYSTICISM

The first stage of Mysticism which you are now going to learn is known as the Purgative State. This is achieved through mystic contemplation by sitting in stillness and holding your mind on certain states of consciousness.

The Purgative State of meditation and contemplation is to be used for the following purposes:

1. To purify your mind of life's erosive forces.
2. To refine your emotions and sensibilities.
3. To overcome human tendencies to immorality, lust, uncontrolled passions and animalism.
4. To discipline the mind and body and bring them under perfect control.

REGIMEN TO ACHIEVE THE PURGATIVE STATE OF MYSTICISM

1. To achieve this purifying state of mysticism, sit in a place where you will not be disturbed for at least one hour. Use the sacred mantra from Tibet, *Aum mane padme aum,* which means, the jewel in the heart of the lotus. You can also chant other mantras to achieve various stages of meditation. A mantra

is a word or short sentence which is repeated over and over, until its full power has been registered upon the higher mind centers. Such words as peace, joy, good, love, truth, beauty and God, may also be used as one-word Mantras for purposes of meditation.

2.   To go into the first stage of meditation, sit quietly with your hands in the prayer position in front of your chest. Breathe deeple five times, being aware of the purifying effect of the breath on your mind and body. This is the Celestial fire or Prana that cleanses the bloodstream, removing all the toxins and impurities from the system and supplanting the blood with new, life-giving oxygen and cosmic energy.

3.   Now, repeat the Sacred Mantra from Tibet five times; *Aum mane padme aum.* As you say these syllables softly, let the hum rise gently into the head region, with your eyes closed and the lips closed, you will feel the humming sensation in the mask of the face. This mystical mantra is helping open the psychic centers, the third eye that is located in the head area called the Seventh Chakra.

Now you can open your eyes and read the following meditation statements. When you acquire greater proficiency in the art of meditation you can make up your own meditations, or memorize these:

I now enter into a state of meditation for purposes of spiritual, mental and physical purification.

I contemplate on my mind, the power behind the throne of my physical and material life.

I remove all negative emotions of fear, worry, hate, greed, selfishness, envy, revenge and lust from my consciousness. I now supplant these negative emotions and thoughts with the positive forces of good, peace, joy, love, beauty, truth and charity.

I now open my psychic third eye and am aware of the world of invisible phenomena. I sit in the stillness and attune my soul to the soul rhythm of the universe. I see the beauty that God has created in the universe. I now pattern my thoughts and my emotions after the pattern of God's tapestry of dreams.

Testimony No. 23

Therese H. Overcame Family Problems

Therese H. came into our work in Mysticism with some very severe problems that threatened to undermine her mental and physical health.

Therese could not get along with her family. She fought constantly with her three children, her husband and in-laws. She worried over trifles and never had peace of mind. She constantly had negative thoughts about the terrible things that might happen to her and her family. She visualized accidents and disasters and lived in perpetual fear. It was in this state of mind that Therese sought our spiritual and mystical work and asked me to help her.

I explained to Therese that she was creating her own mental world or horror and discord. I told her that we all have the power to live in minds filled with confusion and unhappiness, or we can change that condition into one of harmony and peace.

I then gave Therese the meditations and mantras that are given above and told her to stop several times a day and read the entire meditation statement for purification of her mind and emotions. Then she was to repeat one word meditations whenever she found herself troubled by any life situation. She would chant the mantra *Peace* five to ten times. Or she would chant the mantra *Love*, when she found herself hating her in-laws. When her mind dwelt on tragedy and impending disaster, she was to chant the Mantra *God is Good. God is Love.* Then she would say the following meditation statement:

> *I am enclosed in the magic circle of God's protective love and no harm can come near me. I radiate love and forgiveness to everyone I meet. I am joyous and radiate happiness in every situation in my life experience.*

These mystic meditations, chants and mantras soon began to work miracles in Therese's life. She soon found that she was able to control her mind and her emotions. She felt a deep sense of inner peace and calm, which she had never been able to attain before. Soon, her children reacted differently and were more obedient and well-behaved. Even her husband and his relatives changed their attitudes towards Therese and began to show her the respect and love that she desired. Her problems were soon ended and Therese was living a happy and fulfilled life.

HOW TO ACHIEVE THE SECOND
STAGE OF MYSTICISM

The second stage of Mysticism, which you are now going to use, is known as the Meditative Stage. The purpose of this particular form of meditation is to attune your mental and spiritual wavelengths to the cosmic rhythm and soul vibration. This form of mysticism yokes you to the God-mind that is in the universe and permits you to have perpetual contact with the guiding voice of intuition and psychic perception.

You can use the Meditative state of Mysticism for the following purposes:

1. To permanently yoke your mind and soul to the cosmic mind, which man calls God.

2. To give you instant psychic perception so that you can be guided through the divine voice of intuition. This means you will develop the gifts of clairvoyance and clairaudience, you will have the power of precognition, the ability to know your future. You can read the soul's akashic record telling you of your past lives and why you are having karma that makes you suffer and how to overcome this negative karma with spiritual therapy.

3. To heal your body if you should become sick and to keep it healthy and strong for one hundred years or more.

4. To attune your mind and soul to the pulsating rhythm of divine love, so that you can find happiness in the romantic state.

REGIMEN TO ACHIEVE THE MEDITATIVE STAGE OF MYSTICISM

1. Upon awakening in the morning, you can begin the process of yoking yourself to the power of the Absolute, which is the creative spirit of God, in His universe. The word Yoga itself literally means to be yoked to the power of God. Meditation is the mystical process of bringing about a closer union with the power behind the universe. A famous mystic of the Far East said, "Meditation takes you to the threshold of God, prayer takes you beyond."

The first words on your lips when you awaken in the morning should be, "Thank you God, for another day of life." Then you should breathe deeply five times, being aware of your breath. This was the first gift that God gave you when you were born. As you become conscious of your breath, you will now say the following meditation statement to keep you yoked to the source of your life and power all day:

"I am now aware of my breath, the gift of life that God gave me. All day today each breath shall ascend to the celestial heights as a prayer of thanksgiving to God for life, for my good health, and for my prosperity. I dedicate my breath as a living prayer to God. I dedicate my mind as a channel to receive God's divine guidance. I dedicate my body as a holy chalice to serve God and to serve humanity. I dedicate my soul as a perpetual reflector of His divine love, His infinite peace, His infinite good and His infinite intelligence.

BECOME YOKED TO THE POWER
OF THE ABSOLUTE FOR A PERFECT
LIFE

2. Several times during each day, you can instantly go into a state of meditation by simply being aware of your breath and thinking "I am now yoked to the power of the Absolute." Stop whatever you are doing several times a day and give yourself a breathing rest period, in which you breathe deeply and hold the breath for a count of four, then exhale on the count of four. This will help raise your mental and physical energy levels and remove the toxins that have built up in your mind and body from stresses that occur in your work or your home.

3. Sometime during each day there should be a period that you set aside for Meditation. Preferably this should be in the same area each day; you can set aside a little corner in your home, which you make your altar. You can have a white candle burning, incense will give a pleasant aroma, and soft lights will aid the meditation techniques. When you have prepared your simple shrine, you are ready to go into the second stage of Meditative Mysticism.

4. Sit with your eyes closed and do the mystic mantra from Tibet five times. *Aum mane padme aum.* Pronounce the AUM as OHM.

5. Now mentally visualize your mind as being a still lake on a bright summer day. See the golden sun and the blue skies reflected in the lake. Try to still your mind now so that there are no ripples on the mental lake. These ripples are caused by the negative emotions, which the Mystics call earth hinderances. These are fear, worry, hate, greed, envy, jealousy, selfishness, lust, miserliness and animalism.

6. As the lake reflects the sun and sky, so too your mental lake now reflects the eternal golden light of God's presence. Your soul, now serene and calm, reflects the divine intelligence and infinite beauty of the eternal soul of the universe, which is God reflected in his creation. Hold this inner stillness and hold this image of God's presence reflected in your mind and soul.

MEDITATION FOR PEACE OF
MIND AND HARMONY

7. Now you can read the following meditation statement;

I am now yoked to the absolute power behind the universe. My mind is as calm and still as a quiet lake on a peaceful summer's day.
I now push all the ripples caused by the earth hinderances, down in-

to the body of the lake, until the lake is smooth, serene and calm.
I now reflect God's goodness and divine love. I become peaceful and tranquil. No outer winds of misfortune can disturb the celestial rhythm that exists within my soul.

8.   When you have achieved this state of meditation where you are peaceful and calm, you are ready to open the psychic centers and release the power of your intuitive third eye. Direct your concentration to the center of your forehead and mentally see the picture of an actual eye. Now direct your concentration on this area as you say the following statement to yourself:

I now direct the pranic life energy to my psychic third eye. I ask for divine guidance and the gifts of clairvoyance, clairaudience and prophecy. I attune my psychic mind centers to the cosmic intelligence that possesses all wisdom and knowledge. I ask that this power now guide me in every situation in life.

9.   After this meditation, hold the stillness for at least five or ten minutes. Keep your eyes closed during this development period of psychic phenomena. When you have practiced this form of meditation for several days, you can then be prepared for the next step in the development of psychic power.

WRITE DOWN THE THINGS YOU WANT YOUR PSYCHIC MIND TO DO FOR YOU

10.   The next time you go into meditation to utilize your psychic gifts, write down on a sheet of paper the things that you want this higher psychic mind to do for you. The list might look like this but you can make your own, consisting of the actual revelations you want your psychic mind to make about your future:

- I wish to be guided to the events that make up my future.
- I desire information about the work I should do.
- I ask for guidance as to how I can make the sum of $100,000 for future security.
- Should I buy this house that I am now considering?
- If not, I ask to be guided to the right house. Show me how I can solve the problems that exist in my present life.
- Is this person that I am considering marrying my true soul mate? If not, guide me to the finding of my romantic life partner.

- Where did I lose the valuable piece of jewelry?
- Can I trust this person in my present business deal?
- Is it safe to take this trip at the present time?
- How can I be healed of this illness?
- Reveal to me my soul's akashic record, and let me know the Karmic demerits that my soul has built up over the past reincarnations.
- How can I overcome my Karma and be free of pain, sickness, poverty and unhappiness?

11.   When you have developed your own psychic powers through practicing this second stage of Meditative Mysticism, you will have astounding revelations come through. You can then take any problems into the meditation sessions and ask for solutions. The answer may not come through in that session but if you go about your regular day's activities, your psychic mind will suddenly prompt you to do something that brings about the solution of the problem.

Testimony No. 24

Priscilla A. Attracted Her Soul Mate Through This Method

Priscilla A. had studied meditation techniques in our classes and lectures. She followed the above instructions for developing her psychic third eye and went into meditation each day for a period of half an hour. One day she wrote down on the piece of paper she took with her into meditation the following request:

I desire meeting my true soul mate. I wish to be guided to the finding of my right work. I ask for a solution to my life's problems. I need the sum of $1,000 for immediate use.

Each day she went into meditation and read the above requests. She projected to her higher psychic centers these requests and had complete confidence that they would be granted.

For a few days nothing seemed to happen. Her life went on as usual. Then, one day, she had lunch with a girl friend and the friend told Priscilla about a wonderful new beauty parlor where she had her hair done each week. That was all, nothing especially revealing about it, but something in Priscilla's psychic mind centers clicked, and when she had an appointment for a job, she decided to have her hair done at the new beauty salon.

I will let her tell what happened, in her own words, just as she told it to me.

The moment I stepped into that beauty parlor I felt a strange sense of something important happening to me. I was assigned to a booth by the hostess and waited a few moments. Then a very handsome man of about thirty, with auburn hair and blue eyes, stepped into the booth and introduced himself to me. I did not think of anything unusual happening but I kept feeling that I was in the right place and that this young man, whose name was Glenn would do a good job on my hair. As Glenn worked, he talked to me in a charming, cultured voice that I felt belonged to a man of sensitivity and good background. I did not fall in love with him at that session, but I did have a feeling that I would return again and I wanted him to become my permanent hairdresser.

Two weeks later Priscilla told me she had an irresistible urge to return to the beauty salon, and this time something happened that made her feel Glenn was more than casually interested in her. She found out that he owned the beauty salon and he asked her if she would go out on a dinner date with him the following week. As though in a dream, she found herself saying "Yes" and it was in that moment that the psychic revelation came to Priscilla, "This is the man you are going to marry!"

Sure enough, one date led to another; Glenn told her that he had been married and divorced and the moment he saw her he felt something drawing them together. He proposed marriage and within three months from the time Priscilla had made her request from her higher psychic mind centers, she was happily married to Glenn. But the best part was still to come; Priscilla was given the job as hostess in the beauty salon, and she was able to work side by side with the man who turned out to be her perfect soul mate. Obviously, as it turned out, she had an income from the increased business that solved all of her financial worries. Each request she had made of the Higher Cosmic Mind, through meditation, was granted in a short period of three months!

12. You can take into your psychic meditation sessions other requests and ask for information and guidance about various things that you desire.

Testimony No. 25

Morton E. Lost More Than 40 Pounds Through Guidance

Morton E. had a terrific weight problem and needed to lose forty pounds. He suffered from high blood pressure, his heart gave him problems and it was imperative he do something to improve his health.

Morton took into his daily meditation sessions the following written request:

How can I overcome this weight problem? Show me how to master my blood pressure and heart condition.

One day he sat in his doctor's office waiting to take a cardiogram, he thumbed through a magazine on the table, and found an ad that was about a new diet that would guarantee to take off his excess weight. He jotted down the name and address, and later sent for the literature about the new diet. Somehow he had faith in this new diet, although nothing had ever worked for him in the past.

The outcome of this intuitive guidance was that Morton went on the new diet and in three months' time had lost more than forty pounds. The amazing thing was that he suffered no hunger pangs and felt no great strain, as he had with other diets. It's possible that Morton's higher psychic mind centers were programming his body chemistry so that any diet he would have undertaken at that time would have had the same results! When this higher mind takes over it guides you to the right foods to eat and the right methods to use to keep your body healthy. The result on Morton's health was immediate and when he lost his weight, his blood pressure dropped to normal and he no longer suffered from his former heart condition.

HOW TO ACHIEVE THE THIRD
STAGE OF MYSTICISM

The third stage of Mysticism is known as the state of spiritual ecstasy or the blending with the light. This is also referred to by the mystics of the East as the finding of Nirvana. Sometimes, advanced Mystics refer to this third stage of Mysticism as Entering the Golden Door of Brahma. One of the evidences of success in achieving this last stage of Mysticism is that the person experiencing it becomes spiritually illumined. It is then that Cosmic Consciousness dawns and one becomes an Illumined Master.

The third stage of mysticism gives the following benefits:

1. It reveals the true spiritual reality behind life.
2. It helps remove the shadows cast by mortal mind and matter, such as sickness, fear, worry, hate, war, poverty and pain. By turning on the light of spirit, these dark shadows instantly disappear.
3. It reveals the true nature of God and attunes the individual's soul to the Cosmic Soul or spirit behind creation.
4. It helps focus the mind on the true spiritual treasures in the universe, such as health, happiness, peace, love, friendship, beauty in nature and the soul's serenity.

REGIMEN TO ACHIEVE THE THIRD STAGE OF MYSTICISM

1.   To achieve Spiritual Ecstasy through the third stage of mysticism, you can go into a daily meditation session as you did for the other two stages of Mysticism:

1. Have a white candle burning at your sacred shrine. You can also have incense to give a pleasant aroma. Have the lights dimmed.
2. Now with your hands folded as in prayer, say the sacred Mantra from Tibet, *Aum mane padme aum*, five times. Breathe deeply, being aware of breath as the Celestial fire that radiates throughout your body bringing you into attunement with the Cosmic Spirit, which man calls God.
3. You can now read the following Meditation for achieving spiritual ecstasy, visualizing as you do so, a beautiful Lotus with one thousand and one petals. The Lotus of the Far East was chosen as a spiritual symbol for meditation because of its perfection and beauty. It is very much like our water lily, but bigger and comes in many different shades:

> *I now rise to the very heights of the spiritual mountaintop where I transcend the gravity pull of earth. I rise above the negative forces of life. I lay aside my mortal cloak of physical form and limitation. I take on the immortal raiment of my soul's spiritual reality. I know that I am already a perfect spiritual being, created in the image and*

likeness of God. I cannot be sick, tired or old. I cannot die, as I am immortal. My soul had no beginning and will have no ending.

4. When you have achieved this ascension to the spiritual mountaintop and you are in a state of spiritual ecstasy, you will contemplate the Divine Mystery behind life.

   You will meditate on these spiritual thoughts:
   - Who is God?
   - What is the purpose behind my life?
   - What is the soul?
   - Have I lived before and what is my Karmic Destiny?
   - How can I find the perfect pathway to Heaven?
   - How can I attune my soul to His glorious golden presence?

5. Sit in stillness and let your mind contemplate each of the above questions, one at a time, giving yourself several minutes for each answer. Something will speak to your higher mind centers and you will feel a sense of ineffable peace and tranquility as the spirit speaks to your soul.

6. Many times, as you sit in stillness, after you have opened your higher psychic mind centers, you will receive answers to life's baffling questions or solutions to your problems. Sometimes this will come as a still, small voice, and at other times it will be revealed to you through your own subconscious or conscious mind.

Testimony No. 26

Agatha C. Rebuilt Her Life Through Mysticism

For example, a woman who studied in our classes, named Agatha C. was in a state of constant fatigue. She suffered from numerous aches and pains and took tranquilizers, pep pills, and sleeping pills, all under a doctor's prescription. She had been taking Valium for some months and her condition had gradually become worse. Finally, after her husband had left her because of her erratic actions and strange behavior, she tried to commit suicide. Her mother found her before she died, however, and Agatha was saved.

It was in this condition that she first sought our help in spiritual work.

Agatha needed a great deal of work to help her gain strength enough to overcome the terrible negative patterns she had fallen into. I gave her the three Stages of Meditation, which you have just studied, and within two weeks time, she reported that she was strong enough to stop taking drugs and she could fall into a natural sleep every night, which helped restore her. Her husband saw that she was making great efforts to heal herself and he returned to the home to help her. In another month Agatha had recovered sufficiently to return to her work, and she took up her normal life without ever having a recurrence of the deadly affliction that had nearly destroyed her life.

Testimony No. 27

Wendy T. Used Mysticism to Overcome Prostitution

Another instance of extreme need was that of Wendy T., who had a miserable childhood. She had been orphaned early in life, suffered cruel punishments in an orphanage and was then adopted by people who were religious fanatics and punished her for all kinds of fancied sins. Wendy ran away from her adopted parents' home at the age of fifteen and fell in with a man who turned her into a prostitute. The next few years were a nightmare existence for this sensitive young woman, and it was through a friend of hers that she learned she could be helped through our studies.

Wendy began to use all three stages of Mysticism with the meditations given above, and she responded instantly to the powerful spiritual forces that began to work in her mind and spirit. I am happy to say she was completely healed of her many negative conditions and soon obtained a job with a large organization where her naturally brilliant mind won her immediate promotions and a good salary.

MYSTO-MATIC POINTERS

1. *You can use mystical power to project your wishes and desires to others, causing them to do your bidding. Say*

the key words I control seven times. Then repeat the following command:

John, I now command you to respond to my wishes and desires for our mutual good.

Then give the command you wish him to obey.

2. *At night, on the astral, you can project your desires to a person such as your boss and command: I now command you to give me a $10 a week raise in salary. Repeat this ten times before going to sleep.*

3. *You can project a magic spell to your love partner commanding more love, loyalty and affection. Do this just before going to sleep.*

4. *You can reach out on the astral to people in distant places, commanding them to write or phone you. Repeat the command ten times.*

5. *If you desire a true soul mate in love, send the astral thought at night: I now project my loving thoughts to my true soul mate and the desire that we shall meet under God's divine guidance.*

6. *If you have met what you think is your true soul mate but the person does not respond, use the following love spell: Chant the person's name and say to yourself: You will respond to the call of love that I now project from my mind, heart and soul.*

7. *You can use astral projection through meditation to ask for large sums of money. Repeat the following ten times: I direct my higher mind to bring me the sum of $100,000 or more for future security.*

8. *If you have problems you wish removed state: I ask my higher mind to assist me in the removal of all problems from my life. It will respond by causing you to take actions that remove these problems.*

6

FOLLOW THE MYSTIC,
NOBLE EIGHTFOLD PATH
TO GREATNESS
AND ACHIEVEMENT

There is a saying in mystic philosophy, "The sun rises in the east and sets in the west." Always, the great spiritual truths that have been revealed to the world have come to us from the eastern mystics, teachers, prophets and seers. The western world has often accepted these great teachings but, in each instance, they have broken them up into various sects and creeds which have dissipated some of the original value of the spiritual teachings revealed by these prophets and seers.

In this chapter, we shall study one of the truly great revelations given to the world by the Buddha of India, who gave to the world the mystic noble eightfold path which can lead man to greatness and achievement. The Buddha was known as the Enlightened One and his teachings form the basis of a philosopy, which has become a religion to three quarters of the people on earth.

The arcane records of the Mystical Brotherhood show that the Christian Mystic Jesus spent several years during his early life in the mystical land of India. We know that in the years that Jesus was missing from Jeruselum, he spent much time in Egypt, and then later, it is believed that he visited India and contacted some of the great teachers of that ancient land.

There is an amazing similarity between the teachings of the Mystic Jesus and those of the Buddha. The Sermon on the Mount, the Beatitudes, the Golden Rule, are all given in much detail in the revelations of the Buddha who came to earth about five hundred years before Jesus.

THE FOUR NOBLE TRUTHS FOR
EMANCIPATION FROM
SUFFERING

Before you learn the mystic noble eightfold path that can liberate you from the earth hinderances and bring you a life of greatness and achievement, you must know that there are four noble truths which give you immediate emancipation from suffering.

These are:

FIRST NOBLE TRUTH
There is suffering in the world and most suffering is caused by man's uncontrolled desires and sensual appetites.

SECOND NOBLE TRUTH
Suffering is caused by man's greed, selfishness, desires and worship of material and physical things.

THE THIRD NOBLE TRUTH
The path to peace of mind and freedom from suffering is achieved through renunciation (this means giving up to a great extent) of the eternal and restless quest for fame and fortune and social honors.

THE FOURTH NOBLE TRUTH
The Buddha called the fourth noble truth "The Way, the Truth and the Life."
This revelation shows a formula for finding peace of mind and fulfillment through seeking the Inner path, the mystical approach to life.

THE MYSTIC, NOBLE EIGHTFOLD
PATH TO GREATNESS

Now you are ready to apply each of the mystic principles that lead you to a finding of the noble eightfold path to greatness and achievement.

1. RIGHT VIEW, OR UNDERSTANDING
2. RIGHT THOUGHT, OR ASPIRATION
3. RIGHT SPEECH
4. RIGHT CONDUCT
5. RIGHT MEANS OF LIVELIHOOD
6. RIGHT ENTERPRISE, OR EFFORT
7. RIGHT MENTAL CONTROL
8. RIGHT MEDITATION AND CONTEMPLATION

HOW TO HAVE THE RIGHT VIEW
OF LIFE OR UNDERSTANDING

See the true reality that is behind life. Each situation you find yourself in is impermanent and will soon pass. This can help free you from the shocks and disappointments that come when you discover you cannot hold onto anything in life. Your children grow up and go out on their own. Your money is never secure; the political scene is always changing, generally for the worse. Age creeps upon us, accidents occur, we lose our jobs, the mortgage on the home never seems to be paid off, money never quite goes far enough and we can always use more and more.

FIND LIFE'S TRUE REALITY
WITHIN YOUR CONSCIOUSNESS

The Buddha taught that the only true reality that ever exists is within your own consciousness. You can shape and mold your personal life in the image and pattern of the things you hold as reality. You substitute spiritual reality for outer reality of dimension and form and substance, and then you will know the world of spirit that is unchanging, eternal and immortal.

Your soul becomes the only true spiritual reality. It cannot be poor or sick or die. It is eternally youthful and knows its ultimate destiny of glory and elevation. As the butterfly within the cocoon, when it reaches the chrysalis stage, knows that it is to one day emerge as a golden-winged butterfly, so too, man's immortal soul feels the stirring of the wings of the butterfly that will one day be freed from the earth-bound cocoon of sin, sickness, suffering and death to wing its way to the celestial heights and find its true immortality. This is the nirvana that is often referred to by Christians as Heaven.

Testimony No. 28.

Rita Y. Found the Right Understanding

Rita Y. had suffered reversals of fortune and such bitter disappointments in life that she felt she had nothing more to live for. She turned to our studies in mysticism as a last resort, to see if she could find a way out of her tragedies and suffering.

Her first child was born retarded and now, at the age of six, he needed so much care and attention that she hardly had time for her other two children, a boy and girl. To make matters worse, her husband could no longer face up to his responsibilities and deserted her. Rita had gone on welfare, as she could not work and care for her children. She finally yielded to pressure of relatives and placed her retarded son in a public institution. Also, Rita suffered from many different forms of illness, most of them induced by the pressures of life. She got up more tired than when she went to bed. She dragged her body through each day with dread and actual physical pain. Nothing seemed to help her, so she sought out our work to see what could be done for her.

The first thing I had Rita do was change her mental viewpoint or understanding of her life. Her preconditioned mental attitude that she was born to suffer, that her child, who was retarded, was in some way suffering because of her sins, and that she could never rise above her problems and life karma, these negative viewpoints had already doomed her to a life of poverty, sickness and misery.

MEDITATION FOR FINDING THE
SOUL'S REALITY

I gave Rita the following meditation to use so that she could obtain a different understanding of her life situation. She was to do this meditation three times a day:

I am now aware of my soul's true reality. I know that life is transitory and suffering exists in the physical and material realm. I now rise above this world of solid reality into the spiritual stratosphere where the soul resides in perfect peace and bliss. I now see the reality of good, not evil, in my life. I now see the reality of beauty, not ugliness. I create a mental atmosphere of optimism, not pessimism. I know that my life can change and reflect love happiness, not hate and discontent.

Very soon, after she began to use this meditation to obtain the right view or understanding of her life situation, Rita began to change. As her consciousness became illumined, her seemingly hopeless situation seemed less burdensome and she was soon able to find work that made her self-supporting. She met a man who fell in love with her at her work, and they married. The spiritual reality that Rita had projected through the above meditation became the outer reality of her life and she was at last peaceful, healthy and happy.

HOW TO HAVE THE RIGHT
THOUGHTS, OR ASPIRATIONS

Your right thoughts and aspirations must consist of knowing life's true values and then aspiring to achieve them. Each day go over your thoughts and check them to see if they are causing you confusion and problems. Do you basically set a money value on everything in life? If so, then you are apt to be unhappy most of the time. Some people measure their content or discontent in life with whether they do or don't have sufficient money in the bank to make them feel secure.

It is good to have a sense of money value, for money can buy most of the things in life that give comfort, health and security, but money must not be thought of as absolutely essential to peace of mind and happiness.

Have high aspirations to give you strong motivation in life. Have a desire to help your family to a better way of life, educate your children, to bring peace to the world, to create beauty for others to enjoy. These high aspirations will cause you to build a better world for yourself and for others.

HOW TO USE THE RIGHT SPEECH
TO MOTIVATE YOUR LIFE

1.   Today, more than ever before, scientists realize that the speech we habitually use stamps our lives with an indelible pattern that reveals to the outer world what we are within. Emerson said, "What you are speaks so loudly that I cannot hear what you say."

Our outer personalities and actions are determined by the patterns of speech we employ. If we habitually think and speak in a positive, successful manner, we automatically take on the attitudes of success and our actions follow suit.

2. Each day make it a point to declare, "This will be my best day. Only good shall come to me today."

3. When you meet other people show your positive attitude towards life by using positive, happy, optimistic and cheerful words.

4. Avoid using words that kill energy and enthusiasm, such words as, Fail, sick, poor, unhappy, bad, hate, and other words that denote negative states of consciousness should be avoided in daily conversation.

5. When talking to those you wish to win or influence, use positive words that encourage and inspire them. Avoid criticizing them or discouraging them, even if you feel that they may be doing something wrong. You can help them more with a positive statement than one that kills their dreams or inspiration.

6. Practice speaking before a mirror so you can learn how to present your ideas to others with poise and conviction.

Testimony No. 29

Bruce T. Used the Right Speech for Success

A real estate salesman, Bruce T., who was rather shy and not too successful, came to me for advice. I gave him a pattern of speech which he was to practice before his mirror each day for two weeks. In this speech, he was telling the would-be purchaser of a home why he should buy that house. He used only positive words in that rehearsed speech. He was told to believe in what he was saying.

Within the next two weeks, Bruce began to sell more houses than formerly. He finally became one of the best salesmen in his office and doubled his income!

HOW TO USE RIGHT CONDUCT TO SHAPE YOUR DESTINY

1. The Ten Commandments have given civilization a code under which man can live in peace and prosperity. The spiritual laws that exist in the universe

determine what is right or wrong conduct. We know that if we steal, or lie and cheat, something in life will punish us. If our conduct is high and moral and we live under the right spiritual laws, then we are rewarded by being healthy, happy, peaceful and prosperous.

2.   Your conduct towards your fellowmen should be governed by the spiritual revelation called The Golden Rule. This means that you shall do unto others as you would have them do unto you. The Golden Rule was given to the world in the revelations of the Buddha and then five hundred years later, repeated in the teachings of Christ.

3.   Right conduct also applies to the rules of morality and decency. Today, we see a great laxity in this moral code. The institution of marriage is threatened, thousands of children are born out of wedlock and denied the love of parents. Society is undermined by these forces of modern permissiveness. A return to the old-fashioned standards of morality and decency is essential if we are to survive as a race.

Testimony No. 30

How Lillian D. Overcame Tragedy Through Mysticism

An instance of how suffering can be brought about when this rule of right conduct is violated, was that of Lillian D. who was twenty-two years of age. She came into our work a very unhappy young lady. She had fallen in love with a young man who urged her to have a trial marriage by living together first. He promised that after six months time they would be married, if all went well.

During that time, Lillian became pregnant and the young man did not want to have a child, so he urged her to have an abortion. Her parents, being religious, objected and put up a struggle that finally alienated Lillian from them. She had the abortion and then suffered such guilt feelings that she began to hate the young man.

At the end of the six month period, the young man left her and went to live with another young woman and Lillian felt so miserable she wanted to die. An attempt at suicide was foiled and she recovered in the hospital, a bitter and disillusioned young woman. She went back to her family and tried to renew her life again. She began a study of Mysticism in our group and in few weeks time her mental and spiritual wounds were healed. She is now on the road to complete recovery and has found a fine young man who wants marriage and a family.

HOW TO USE THE RIGHT MEANS
OF LIVELIHOOD

1. The Buddha taught that we must all work and be useful, or our lives are apt to fall into periods of boredom and discontent. Find work that you enjoy, for one third of your life will be spent in productive activity.

2. Do not think any honest work is demeaning or beneath you. Lincoln started life as a rail splitter; Carnegie was a poor boy from Scotland, and worked as a laborer in steel mills learning the trade that later made him millions. No work is demeaning, but if you are in work you do not like, you must study something else until you are able to find your right work.

MONEY OBEYS CERTAIN COSMIC
LAWS

3. Do not think that you can get something for nothing or that you will get rich overnight. Money obeys certain cosmic laws and can only be obtained by exchanging your labor or your creative ideas for something of value, either money or goods.

4. Get as much education as you can. If forced to leave school early by circumstances beyond your control, enroll in evening high school and take courses in studies that interest you.

5. Remember, from the neck down, as a laborer, a man is worth only a few dollars a day, but from the neck up, in the realm of the mind and ideas, a man can be worth millions. Try to rise into the realm of creative ideas in your work so you can give greater benefits to humanity and also enrich yourself.

HOW TO USE RIGHT ENTERPRISE
OR EFFORT TO IMPROVE YOUR
LIFE

1. This principle relates to the value that one sets on achievement or effort that one makes to win a goal in life. One might ask: Is it the making of the million dollars that brings a person enjoyment or is it the million dollars itself? The Buddha taught that if one makes the right effort to win life's high goals and rich rewards, and lives according to the spiritual laws, it is not vitally important if a person achieves his goal or not. If a person enjoys his work and if he contributes to the betterment of the world and is honest in his endeavors, such a person is more successful than one who wins world-wide acclaim and riches, but who may be miserable in his personal life.

2.   Many people say one can only become rich by being dishonest. It seems true that such people often rise to high places but soon the law of Karma takes over and they suffer loss and privation because of their dishonesty. Al Capone may have built a fortune through his dishonest methods but he became sick and was imprisoned because of his evil actions.

3. There are ten virtues that were given by the Buddha, which you can apply to your own life. These are:

Honesty, truthfulness, goodness, justice, mercy, compassion, idealism, forgiveness, charity and love.

When these ten virtues are applied to your life, then every enterprise or effort will be rewarded with success and eventual fulfillment.

HOW TO APPLY THE RIGHT
MENTAL CONTROL TO YOUR LIFE

1.   The Buddha discovered a great psychological principle, that modern science now confirms. It is that the control of one's thoughts and emotions is one of life's great accomplishements. Watch the thoughts that you permit to enter your mind. If these thoughts are negative, fearful, hateful, worrisome and selfish, they will reflect in your outer actions and color you life with negativity.

2.   Each day, check your thoughts at the door of the mind, be sure that only happy, healthy, successful and positive thoughts are allowed to enter your consciousness.

HOW TO RESTORE PEACE AND
SERENITY TO A TROUBLED MIND

3.   To clear your mind of these negative thoughts from the past, sit in quiet meditation and visualize your mind as a peaceful, quiet lake. Then, as you consciously think a disturbing thought, such as fear of an accident or worry about a debt, this negative thought will cause a ripple on the surface of your mental lake. As your thoughts become more negative and uncontrolled, this ripple becomes a giant wave until the surface of your mental lake is completely turbulent and can no longer accurately reflect the outer world of reality.

4.   Now you can restore peace and serenity in your mental lake by pushing each disturbing wave or thought, down into the body of the lake, until the surface of the lake is once again calm and tranquil.

5. Control your thoughts each day by having practice sessions of meditation in which you choose a positive thought for that day. One day choose the thought of peace. All that day you will remind yourself to be peaceful and calm. The next day, choose Beauty. Try to think beautiful thoughts all day and to see beauty in your environment, not ugliness. Another day choose the emotion of happiness and search for happy events all day. In this way you will soon train yourself to control your thoughts and perpetually be in a state of balance and harmony.

HOW TO HAVE THE RIGHT
MEDITATION AND
CONTEMPLATION

1. A great deal of time is spent in mystic philosophy in meditation and contemplation. This is sometimes called spiritual ecstasy or rapture in the Buddha's teachings. It is in meditation that one reaches the highest state of consciousness that the human mind may achieve.

2. You should go into a quiet meditation at least once a day, although it is possible to do a quick form of meditation several times a day.

3. Before going into meditation, you can recite the mystical mantra used in India and Tibet, which is *Aum mane padme aum*. This means the jewel in the heart of the lotus, and relates to the soul that reflects the divine presence within man.

4. Then close your eyes after intoning the mystical mantra five times and give yourself a silent meditation, using words that you can make up, or a memorized ritual such as the following:

> *I am now peaceful and calm. I am yoked to the absolute power behind life. I reflect the presence of God in my soul. I relax and let the presence work through my mind, my body and my emotions. My soul now pulsates with the soul of the universe and I am in harmony with all the forces behind time and space.*

HOW TO USE CONTEMPLATION
TO BRING SPIRITUAL
PERCEPTION

5. Contemplation is a little different from meditation; it is to think deeply about something, or to ponder over some specific subject, and it can be indulged in daily to bring you greater comprehension and spiritual perception.

6.   On one day, you can contemplate the mind in all its aspects; conscious, subconscious and superconscious mind. Letting your mind dwell on each state of consciousness, many new and interesting revelations will come through to you.

7.   On another day, you can contemplate the body; see its miraculous workings, affirm it's state of good health, youthful vitality and longevity.

8.   On still another day, you can contemplate your emotions, affirming the positive emotions of faith, hope, charity, love, optimism, courage, forgiveness, goodness and idealism.

9.   On the next day, you can contemplate the mystery of your soul, the nature of God, and the true purpose behind your life.

This regimen for seeking out the mystic noble eightfold path to achievement and greatness will work miracles in your life. Apply these principles to your life from now on and you will see the transformation that will take place.

MYSTO-MATIC POINTERS

1. *In applying the principle of renunciation, remember, this does not mean giving up all ambition in life. You can win the White House but don't expect it to last forever. Ambition should be used judiciously so as not to induce suffering.*

2. *The Inner Mystic Path or the Way as the Buddha called it, means living a great deal in the world of the mind, in the realm of ideas and concepts, rather than material and physical things.*

3. *Control your desires and appetites, do not let them control you. It is all right to have normal desires for wealth, success, happiness and love but do not let any of these get out of control.*

4. *In finding the mystic path, learn to spend a great deal of time in mystic meditation and contemplation on the permanent values of life. These include art, music, literature, philosophy and wisdom in general.*

5. *Live under the Golden Rule and the Ten Commandments and you will find the inner pathway to peace and contentment.*

6. *Work out your negative Karma by doing kind acts and being loving, forgiving and understanding of others.*

7. Build your positive Karma in this lifetime by being aware of your weaknesses and then work to correct these. Good overcomes evil; love overcomes hate; charity overcomes selfishness.

8. Do not be ashamed of any work that is honest. Look on your present work as a stepping stone to greatness.

9. Realize that this world is a testing ground for your soul; meet life's challenges with poise and equanimity.

7

RELEASE PYRAMID POWER
FOR A GREAT
NEW LIFE OF
SUPER-ABUNDANCE

Today, more than ever before, the entire world is interested in the great
pyramids of Egypt. Built by the ancient Pharaoh Cheops, the great pyramid at
Giza was built about 3000 B.C. The other pyramids were begun by the kings of
Egypt at Sakkara. Throughout the ages they have stood as symbols of mystery
and strange powers.

Now modern scientists believe that the pyramid form is capable of giving
out a mysterious type of energy which can be harnessed and utilized to perform
seeming miracles.

In chapter one you were given the initiation ceremony used by the ancient
Egyptians to bring about a complete rebirth in consciousness. Now, you will be

taken a step further in using the mystical rituals and invocations to release vast stores of latent psychic energy within your higher mind, so you can instantly begin to benefit from the use of Pyramid Power.

This chapter will disclose the various forms of Pyramid Power and show you how to channel this awesome energy for health, power and a life of super-abundance.

MYSTICAL AND ESOTERIC
SYMBOLOGY IN THE PYRAMIDS

Since the discovery of the Rosetta stone, which gave the key to the hieroglyphics, the picture writing used by the ancient Egyptians, many of the Egyptian secrets have been learned by modern scientists. We now know that the pyramids were filled with mystical and esoteric symbology and were built according to astrological knowledge that was greater than that possessed by modern astronomers. In fact, finely ground lenses were recently found in the King's chamber in the Pyramid of Giza that scientists say could only have been made by machines!

Predictions that have been found in the carvings of the walls of the Pharaoh's tombs in the Valley of the Kings, are said to be amazingly accurate and have prophesied events that take us right up to our modern age of atomic energy. In fact, one of these picture-writings foretells that in the Aquarian age a ball of fire comes from the west, which could entirely destroy all civilization. This undoubtedly refers to the atomic bomb.

STRANGE POWERS POSSESSED BY
THE MIND OF MAN

The ancient Egyptians believed that the human mind possessed strange and unusual powers. They taught that the mind could set vibrations into motion that would act upon the molecules and atoms of creation, bringing about profound changes in the structure of matter and the materialization of new and unusual products. We have seen this in our modern age of science where man has split the atom, releasing the power of a thousand suns, and in the creation of new products like plastics, artificial building materials, cloth, foods and synthetic products which have changed the face of the earth in modern times.

The ancient Egyptians believed in the soul and its survival after life. They taught that the world was constructed of three primary forms; a dome, a block or square and a pyramid.

These three primary forms were further broken down into what they called *rays* The first ray is shown as a circle with a dot inside. This undoubtedly relates to procreation, wherein the male cell penetrates the female cell to begin the mystical process of life.

The second ray was shown as a cross, which represents the balance that all elements must maintain.

The third ray was shown as a triangle or pyramid shape, representing the mystical triplicity of man, God and the universe. In the Chrisitian religion we also have this mystical trinity, the Father, Son and Holy Ghost. In psychology, this symbol represents the conscious, the subconscious and the superconscious minds.

The fourth ray was shown as two pyramids together, one turned upside down on the other. This symbol is used by some fraternal organizations. When the lines of these two pyramids are joined together they form the picture of the Star of David, utilized by the ancient Jewish Faith.

The fifth ray was shown as a pyramid on top of a square.

The sixth ray was pictured as four interlocked circles. A modified form of this sixth ray has been used as the Grecian Olympic games symbol.

The seventh ray was shown as a swastika, which was used by the Indian tribes of North America as their national symbol.

MYSTICAL RITES IN THE TEMPLE OF OSIRIS

The ancient Egyptians were great believers in magic. They taught that man is made up of the same elemental forces that were used in building the universe from these seven astral rays. They performed mystical rites in the temple of Osiris in which they invoked the elements of air, fire, earth and water to perform miracles. We see this reflected in the miracles of Jesus, the Christian mystic, when he turned water into wine. He also proved the conquest of the human mind over the elements when he performed His amazing miracle of walking upon the troubled waters. He was able to feed the multitudes with the loaves and fishes, proving the magical power of materialization of substance from the very air. He healed the sick by transforming the sickly body cells into healthy, living matter. These great feats were all proofs that a magical power does exist in the universe and that man may also tap this hidden, mystical power for his own living miracles.

THE MIRACULOUS GUSHING
FOUNTAIN IN THE EGYPTIAN
DESERT

When I was in Egypt recently, with a group of seventy people, we visited the shrine that has been set up where Jesus and the Holy Family lived, after they fled into Egypt to avoid persecution. There, in the basement of that Holy Chapel, in the midst of a desert, near the great Pyramid of Giza, a fountain of water gushed up and is still flowing copiously after nearly two thousand years! The element of water is symbolic of the spiritual baptism and represents the flow of celestial power from on high when a person is reborn in the consciousness of his own soul's immortality. Miracles have been performed in this sacred spot, where the sick have been healed, and the requests of believers have been granted for health, happiness, money, business and romantic success. This release of Mystical Power is what we shall now experience together in our further study of Pyramid Power for a great new life of super-abundance.

THE RITUAL OF SUN BLENDING
FOR MIRACLE-WORKING POWER

1.   You will now prepare yourself for the ritual of Sun Blending to release miracle working power within your own higher mind centers. The ancient Egyptians were monotheistic and believed in one God. Their religious faith resembled that of modern Christian nations but they used various symbols for their rituals, such as the sun and the moon. They paid honors to a number of Gods but they never placed those Gods on the same high level as the One God, that they worshiped.

As the sun was the symbol of life, energy, health and unlimited power, they used the temple of Osiris to concentrate on the golden sun to give them miracle working powers for healing, rejuvenation, vital life energy, long life, and creative mental activity.

MYSTICAL RITUAL IN THE
TEMPLE OF OSIRIS FOR HEALING

2.   You will now prepare yourself for the Mystical ritual in the temple of Osiris by withdrawing into a quiet center in your own environment, where you will not be disturbed for a period of one hour. Have a picture of a Pyramid, or better still, a small model of a Pyramid in wood or metal or plastic, somewhere

on a table before you as you perform this ritual. Be aware that this Pyramid represents the focusing of all your mental and spiritual energies for the purpose of performing miracles in your own life.

3.   Still your conscious mind with this statement:

I now concentrate all my mental powers on the absorption of Pyramid Power to perform miracles in my own life. I recognize Osiris, the symbol of the sun in our universe. This symbol now releases its life-giving energies and I am bathed in the golden light of the sun. It flows through my mind, body and spirit, releasing its health-restoring, life-giving elements that bring me instant healing.

4.   You are now ready to direct the flow of miracle-working power from the golden spiritual sun that created the universe to your body in order to achieve a perfect healing of any negative condition that may exist. Repeat the following invocation for healing:

I now blend with the golden light of the spiritual sun that is behind the universe. I absorb the healing Celestial Rays of the golden sun and respond to its stimulating, life-giving force. I now blend with the invigorating power of the sun, and I take on its radiant quality of life energy, power and magnetism. I become healed of all bodily afflictions as the life-sustaining power of the sun now flows through every nerve, cell and tissue of my body. I am perfect. I am restored. I am young. I am healthy. I am powerful. I am in the golden magic circle of the power that sustains all life.

Testimony No. 31

Gertrude D. Was Completely Healed With Sun Blending Ritual

One of my lecture members in Los Angeles, Gertrude D., had been sick for some time, and doctors did not seem to be able to help her. She suffered from severe abdominal cramps, particularly at her menstrual cycles each month. She also had low energy and vitality and had to remain in bed for many days, not able to face even her household tasks. Because she had no appetite, she was losing weight to such an extent that it became dangerous to her health. It was at this time that she sought out our studies in mysticism and learned about the Sun blending exercise in the temple of Osiris.

Gertrude began to practice this meditation technique, concentrating on the healing rays of the sun. She absorbed the Pyramid Power that flowed throughout her body as she concentrated on a small metal pyramid that she kept before her while she did her rituals. She said the above Pyramid Power statement several times a day, and soon began to feel more relaxed and stronger physically. Within two weeks time, Gertrude reported that she had more energy than before, and the abdominal cramps had stopped completely. She was soon back at her normal weight and was completely healed.

SUMMON THE POWER OF OSIRIS
TO OVERCOME HABITS SUCH AS
SMOKING

5. You can also use this mystical ritual in the Temple of Osiris for other purposes. You can ask for power to overcome negative habits, to help you gain strength for meeting the challenges of life, to release mental and physical power for prolonged creative efforts in your work. This exercise in sun blending focalizes the golden rays of the sun in your mind and psychic centers and brings about a tremendous increase in your mental and physical powers.

Testimony No. 32

Daryl J. Used Sun Blending to Quit Smoking

A thirty-five year old man, Daryl J., had smoked for fifteen years when he first came into our work. He had tried in every way to stop this dangerous habit, but to no avail. When he discovered the sun blending exercise from the Temple of Osiris, he began using the following Invocation daily for a period of three weeks, and he was soon able to completely stop his harmful habit. Here is the invocation to the sun that Daryl used:

> *I now blend with the golden light of the sun to gain strength of mind and body. I desire to stop the harmful habit of smoking. I know that this habit is dangerous to my health and I sincerely want to stop. I now recognize the power that is symbolized by the purifying rays of the golden sun. I absorb the energy and strength of the sun in my mind and body. I now become strong and determined. I blend with the sun and absorb its healing rays. My higher mind*

centers now are given the strength and determination to stop smoking. I breathe in the life-giving strength of the golden sun and its power now flows through my body in a tidal wave of life and energy, causing me to no longer desire cigarettes. I am healed of this noxious habit.

HOW TO USE PYRAMID MONEY POWER THROUGH SUN BLENDING

6. Pyramid Money Power can be released through the use of this mystical ritual from the Temple of Osiris, known as sun blending.

To use this power to increase your supply of money, sit quietly in meditation, using the symbol of the Pyramid to help you concentrate your creative energies on money.

Mentally visualize the light of the sun streaming earthward, causing all life to grow and evolve. See the products of earth springing up in the spring and summer, blessing humanity with fruits, vegetables, grains and all kinds of products to sustain human life.

ALL EARTH'S TREASURES COME FROM THE POWER OF THE SUN

Realize that the golden sun is responsible for all of the earth's treasures. Lumber to build your dream home comes from the energy of the sun. The coal, oil, diamonds, healing herbs and food products, are evidences that the golden light of the sun is being transformed by the law of Alchemy into all the products we need to sustain us throughout our earthly existence.

Now invoke this power of the golden sun with this invocation for money and the things that money can buy:

I now absorb the golden energy of the sun and receive the creative ideas and inspiration that can bring me an inexhaustible flow of riches and abundance. I invoke the law of Cosmic Alchemy to transform my creative ideas into riches. I magnetize the centers of my consciousness with the power of attraction and project the sum of $50,000, which shall come to me from an unexpected source. I ask for a home of my own, beautiful furnishings in that home, a color TV set, a car of my own, and all other things that I need for

*my future comfort and security. I also wish to have in my bank
account the sum of $50,000 or more to give me future security.*

Testimony No. 33

How Helen F. Used Pyramid Money Power to Attract a Fortune

When Helen F. came into our work in Carnegie Hall, she was so poor that she could hardly buy enough food to feed her two children. Her husband had deserted her after the birth of her second child and she could not locate him, so she had to set to work to pay her own way in life.

Helen began to use the Money Pyramid ritual and sun blending to increase her money supply. Within one week, she obtained a job in a health food store where she learned how much money could be made in that business.

Helen kept projecting the sum of $35,000 in her sun blending exercise each night before she went to sleep. She had no idea where she could ever obtain such a large sum of money. Remember, this was done at a time when money was scarce, not plentiful as it is today with inflation and high costs. But, she had faith that in some way she could attract this sum of money through the use of her mystical powers.

One day, a man came into the health food store and Helen waited on him with courtesy and efficiency. She sold him a great many items, with her super-persuasive sales ability, and the man seemed very impressed. Before he left, he gave her his card and told her to look him up when she had time, as he had an interesting business proposition to make.

The upshot of that chance meeting was that Helen did look this man up and discovered that he was a famous health lecturer and author. When she talked to him, she found out that he wanted to open a health food store with someone he could trust, as he was on the road lecturing and promoting his books. He felt that he had found the right person. He suggested that he put up the sum of $35,000 for capital and that she could give her services, in an equal partnership, in which she would run the business!

Helen received her $35,000 in this most unusual way. They

opened their health food store on Long Island, and soon had such a big business that they had four salespersons working for them, and Helen soon had her own home, a big sum of money in the bank, her own car, and the security for her two children that she had asked for in her invocation and use of Pyramid Money Power.

HOW TO KEEP A STEADY FLOW OF
MONEY COMING THROUGH
PYRAMID POWER

7.   In order to ensure yourself of a steady flow of money through Pyramid Money Power, you can now begin to use the symbol that is given on every dollar bill printed in the United States. Franklin Delano Roosevelt, who was a great student of the occult and mystical, discovered Pyramid Power back in the early 30s when he was President. He had the mystical symbol of the Pyramid printed on the reverse side of every dollar bill, in the middle of a magic circle, which represented the Sun god Osiris.

To utilize this pyramid money power symbol, take a dollar bill, look at the Pyramid on the green side, and then fold the bill in half, with the green side showing. Then fold the two upper corners of the dollar bill back, making a pyramid shape over the printed pyramid on the dollar bill. This now forms a perfect Pyramid.

RITUAL TO PROJECT PYRAMID
MONEY POWER

To project Pyramid Money power, sit quietly in meditation. Hold the folded dollar bill in your hand, with the Pyramid showing. Concentrate your mind on that Pyramid and repeat the following Money Invocation:

> *I now concentrate my mind on Pyramid Money Power. I project a flow of creative mind power to this symbol of money and ask that I be granted a perpetual flow of money, jewels, lands, houses, cars, house furnishings, clothes, and other things of value that I require in my life.*

> *I now project the sum of $5,000 that shall come to me within the next three months' time. I ask for jewelry, and other things of I project a steady flow of money and other treasures that shall enrich my life and give me financial security for the future.*

8.   When you have done the Pyramid Money Power Ritual, you can place the pyramid shaped dollar bill into your purse and each day keep the tip of

it showing in your pocketbook, so every time you spend money you can see this symbol of money power. This will constantly activate your higher mind centers with inspiration to attract large sums of money.

USE THIS MYSTICAL MONEY MANTRA TO ATTRACT MORE MONEY

9.   At least once a day sit in meditation and remind your higher psychic mind centers of this Pyramid Money Power. You can intone the following Meditation Mantras for increasing your supply of money:

I now attract to myself money, money, money.

I become rich and abundantly blessed.

I see a stream of gold flowing into my life.

As the golden sun gives the earth power to produce riches, so too, my mind is now stimulated to creative ideas that will make me rich.

Money, Money, Money, Money, Money, Money.

Testimony No. 34

Marvin P. Used Pyramid Money Power for Security

Marvin P. was a salesman of household furnishings, working in a large store that specialized in refrigerators, vacuum cleaners, TV sets and washing machines. He made a good living but not enough to give him a feeling of financial security for the future of his family of three children.

When Marvin began coming to my classes in Mysticism, he frankly admitted that he wanted to increase his income and be able to own a home, a beautiful new car and other things that he and his wife desired.

In the classes, we studied about Pyramid Money Power and the sun blending exercises to increase one's riches. He began to practice these rituals every night. He also formed the Money Pyramid with his dollar bill. He slept with this under his pillow every night, and also carried one in his wallet every day. He also projected the mental symbol of the third ray, which was the Pyramid, all day when he made his sales in the store. He began to notice immediate benefits. The first week his sales increased by twenty-five percent. Then, in his second week, he won a color TV set at a drawing in his local church. He then began concentrating in earnest on Pyramid Money Power. Within two months time, he had become the most successful salesman in his field and his sales doubled. His commissions were soon twice what they had been before.

He had been driving a shabby, old car, of which he was ashamed. So he began to project the image of a new car and concentrated on the fifth ray picture of a Pyramid on top of a square, which was the symbol of a home. The car came to him within two months' time, and at the end of his first year, he had sufficient money to pay a substantial down payment on his first dream home! Pyramid Money Power began dumping money into his lap from so many other sources that Marvin P. never again felt the financial pinch that had hounded him most of his life.

MYSTICAL RITES IN THE TEMPLE
OF ISIS

Besides the rituals in the Temple of Osiris, the Sun God, the ancient Egyptians performed another amazing ritual in the Pyramids. This took place in the Temple of Isis, and was symbolic of the Moon Goddess.

As the Sun blending in the temple of Osiris represented the masculine qualities of strength, aggression, courage, power and healing, so too, the Moon blending in the temple of Isis was symbolic of the feminine virtues of truth, beauty, peace, love, generosity, kindness, creativity and joy.

RITUAL PERFORMED IN THE
TEMPLE OF ISIS FOR PEACE AND
TRANQUILITY

The neophytes in this ritual of Moon blending performed the following invocation ceremony:

I now concentrate all my mental powers on the absorption of the silvery light of the Moon. The peace and beauty that flow from this celestial orb now fill my mind and soul with infinite peace and radiant beauty.

I now become serene and tranquil as I bask in the silvery light of the full Moon. Its beauty and romance are now reflected in my mind and soul. Its magnetism and power of attraction now cause me to draw into the orbit of my daily experience, the situations and people that benefit my life in every way. I become magnetic and charming.

I attract true love and friendship. I take on the qualities represented by the moon Goddess Isis. These are qualities of truth, beauty, peace, love, generosity, kindness, creativity and joy. My life now flowers with every good and precious gift bestowed upon me by the serene and majestic presence of this beautiful planet, the moon.

Testimony No. 35

How Dorothy B. Used Moon Blending to Change Her Life

A woman I once knew, Dorothy B. who studied these Mystical secrets of Sun and Moon blending, had suffered all her life from feelings of shyness, inferiority and inadequacy. She was not beautiful, and she was not able to attract boys when she was at an age where most girls begin to date. She felt that she was doomed to a life of unhappiness and loneliness, until she discovered Egyptian Pyramid power, as represented by the Moon Blending in the Temple of Isis.

I told her to visualize herself as being an ancient Queen in Egypt, entering the Temple of Isis to invoke the Moon's magnetism and beauty. She was told to believe that the Moon infused her aura with a romantic presence that men would instantly feel. She was then told to do the above ritual of Moon blending, feeling that she was taking on the qualities represented by the Moon Goddess Isis. She added the following invocation statements to her Moon blending exercise:

I am bathed in an aura of majestic beauty. This spiritual aura transcends the physical body and gives me inner beauty and radiance.

I now become a magnet that attracts into my aura the true soul mate that I desire. I walk in the consciousness of beauty, peace and tranquility.

I am loving and kind and others feel the sense of goodness, peace and love that dwells within me.

I now dwell in a radiant circle of charm and enchantment. Everyone who comes into my presence feels this mystical power and reacts with love.

Dorothy practiced this ritual in the temple of Isis every day, twice a day, for only fifteen minutes, and within a few days' time she began to go through an amazing transformation that others instantly noticed.

She carried her head as though wearing a crown; her eyes had an inner glow that seemed to suffuse her features with an inner, translucent beauty that made her face actually look beautiful.

Within a few weeks time, Dorothy was so confident and poised that she began to go out more socially. At a party, in a friend's home, she met a good-looking young doctor who had just begun practicing medicine and he showed an interest in her. He was so intrigued by the aura of mystery and enchantment that Dorothy had, that he asked if he could see her again. Thus began a courtship that later ended in a marriage that brought Dorothy the true soul mate she had asked for in her invocation to Isis.

MYSTO-MATIC POINTERS

1. *Concentrate on the drawing of a circle with a dot in the center and affirm: I am surrounded by the magic circle of God's creative life energy. I move in the direction of my eternal good.*

2. *Concentrate on the second celestial ray of a cross and affirm: I now manifest the cross of balance in all my life affairs. Work is balanced by play; love is balanced by worship of God.*

3. *Concentrate on a small pyramid and affirm: I recognize the spiritual triplicity of Father, Son and Holy Ghost. I become an antenna between heaven and earth receiving cosmic power for good.*

4. *Draw a picture of a pyramid and then on top of this another pyramid upside down, the fourth celestial ray. Now affirm: I recognize the two worlds in which I live, the world of mind and spirit. I now live in the spiritual reality of my life dream.*

5. *Draw a picture of a square and a pyramid on top of the square; affirm: I now contact the cosmic mind that created all things. I ask for divine inspiration to achieve my great goals in life.*

6. *Draw two circles side by side, then one circle on top of these two, and another circle on the bottom. This is the 6th celestial ray. Now affirm: I now dwell in harmony with*

all creation. I have order in my mind and my life shall be orderly, harmonious and prosperous.

7. Withdraw into quiet meditation each day and affirm: I recognize the positive polarity of Good in my life. I draw upon Pyramid power to give me life energy, riches and abundance.

8

REVELATIONS OF ANCIENT CHINESE MYSTICS FOR HEALTHY, HAPPY AND PROSPEROUS LIVING

One of the greatest revelations to come from the Far East is that of the Chinese mystic and philosopher, Confucius. He advised emperors and political leaders, and he formulated a system of codes and ethics, which apply to the twentieth century as much as they did to his era.

Confucius was born in China in 551 B.C. and his true name was K'ung Ch'iu. He was a contemporary of Lao-Tse, and later his disciple was to set forth his own wonderful philosophy in what is called The Pathway to Heaven.

CONFUCIUS USHERED IN THE
GOLDEN AGE OF PHILOSOPHY

It is interesting for a student of mysticism to note that in the golden age of philosophy when Confucius and Lao-tse were giving their mystical truths to China, at the same time in history the Buddha was revealing his Noble eightfold path in India, and in ancient Greece, Pythagoras and Socrates had already appeared and were spreading their brilliant philosophy to the Greeks.

Confucius did not teach a religion as much as a system of philosophy and social progress which could bring order out of chaos and show mankind how to control his natural warmaking and animalistic propensities and desires. He taught that man can make a paradise of this earth if he can bring an orderly system of thinking and acting in relation to the world in which he lives.

Confucius taught that life is in a constant state of flux or change. You cannot hold onto any experience, person, situation or thing. To achieve happiness, you cannot strive to achieve permanency in any relationship in life. You cannot think of any job as being permanent, any marriage as static, any family remaining unbroken, any wealth as secure or any throne of power as eternal.

YIN-YANG PRINCIPLES FOR
PERFECT BALANCE IN LIFE

Once you accept this basic idea of eternal change, you will learn to be in a state of balance between the inner and the outer forces of life. This is called, in mystic philosophy, the balance between Yin and Yang, the two opposing forces in the universe: good and bad; health and sickness; riches and poverty; light and darkness. When this balance is disturbed, the individual is thrown out of tune with the cosmic forces of life and suffers every known type of misfortune and tragedy.

ERADICATE THE 15 SOURCES OF
TROUBLE AND FIND
FULFILLMENT

Confucius taught that there are fifteen main sources of trouble. When these forces of negativity are permitted to rule a person's life, he is robbed of peace of mind, happiness, health and prosperity.

Confucius then indicated a way for overcoming these fifteen sources of trouble. It is by ascending the twelve steps up the Golden Ladder to the pathway to heaven that one finds ultimate peace and security in life.

THE 15 SOURCES OF TROUBLE

1. SELFISHNESS
2. GREED
3. UNCONTROLLED APPETITES AND DESIRES
4. FALSE PRIDE
5. HATE
6. INTOLERANCE
7. ENVY
8. BAD HABITS (such as smoking, drinking and dope addiction)
9. DISHONESTY
10. LIVING IN THE FUTURE OR THE PAST
11. MISERLINESS
12. EXTRAVAGANCE (Living beyond one's means)
13. CRUELTY
14. INJUSTICE
15. MATERIALISM OR LACK OF SPIRITUALITY

TAKE THE 12 MYSTICAL STEPS UP THE GOLDEN LADDER FOR HEAVENLY REWARDS—NOW

1.   First, reason out the causes of your unhappiness. Most people are unhappy because of something they want that they cannot have. This can be the result of a lack of money which makes it impossible to buy a new house, a car, furnishings, jewelry, furs and expensive clothes. If this is the cause of your unhappiness, realize that even millionaries have their worries and problems.

If the source of your troubles is romantic or marital unhappiness, reason out why it is that you cannot get along with your romantic partner, then do something to change yourself or the situation.

IS YOUR UNHAPPINESS DUE TO
THE WRONG WORK?

If your unhappiness is the result of the wrong work, then you can do one of two things: Give up that work and find something else, or study and prepare yourself for a new type of work where you will be happier.

Do not let lack of money be a source of your unhappiness, for even the millionaire desires two million to back up his fortune. Use what you have wisely and avoid living beyond your means. Do not love money but enjoy it and save part of your income for future security. In this way you will never be discontented with your present financial situation but you will constantly be striving to improve it so you may have eventual security.

WHAT YOU CANNOT CHANGE,
LEARN TO LIVE WITH

2. There are many things in life that we cannot change. For instance, you were born to a certain destiny because of your genetic programming. You could not choose your parents, so if you have some situation due to reasons of birth that makes you unhappy and which you cannot change, learn to live with it. You may not be satisfied with the type of face or body nature gave you; your mouth or nose may be too big; you may wish you could have been born to a rich family. This is not always a guarantee of happiness; Patricia Hearst was born to riches but came into tragedy. Use whatever position of birth you have inherited as a stepping stone to greatness.

George Washington Carver was born to slave parents in the South, but he did not let that limit him in his great accomplishments. He became one of the great scientists of the world and created more than twenty different articles from the lowly peanut, including paints, varnishes, food for cattle, insulation material and other valuable products.

DEVELOP YOUR MIND TO ITS
FULLEST POTENTIALS

3. Mind power rules the world. Realize that no matter what limitations you were born into, your mind can be developed to a point where you can rise above life's problems. Study throughout your life. If you were forced to stop school, continue with adult education in evening schools. Take books from the library on many different subjects. Learn a little about psychology, philosophy, science, history, mathematics, art, music, literature, industry and geography.

Gradually, as you develop your mind power you will rise to your full potentials in life and finally achieve a very satisfactory destiny.

REALIZE THAT ALL THINGS ARE
TRANSIENT, SO DO NOT TRY TO
HOLD ONTO ANYTHING
PERMANENTLY

4.   How often people are made miserable because they find they cannot live in the same house forever, or keep their children young, or hold onto their looks, their youth, their fortune or their work. Confucius taught that the only permanent thing we can depend on is CHANGE.

Mystics from the Far East tell us that if the caterpillar stayed forever in the cocoon it would never emerge as a beautiful butterfly. You are constantly evolving into higher stages of consciousness, so use each phase of your development as a necessary part of your spiritual progress and liberation from the earthbound self.

NEVER LET ANY EMOTION
AFFECT YOU SO DEEPLY THAT
YOU ARE PERMANENTLY
SCARRED PSYCHICALLY

5.   All the great mystics taught that men must rise above the emotional realm into the realm of spirituality. If you let every passing wind of misfortune leave its scar on your psyche, you will soon find life burdensome and tortuous. Live fully in all the emotions of joy, love, optimism, hope and goodness, but do not let your emotions get out of control.

Testimony No. 36

Uncontrolled Emotions Made Josephine A. Ill

A case that came to my attention where uncontrolled emotions made one mentally ill was that of Josephine A. She was happily married for fifteen years and had two fine growing children. Suddenly she found out that her husband was being untrue to her. She went into such a rage that she took a butcher knife and tried to stab him! After that she fell into uncontrollable grief and finally became so melancholy that she had to be put into a mental hospital, where she remained for six months under treatment.

When she discovered our work in Mysticism she came for counseling and lessons. She studied these teachings of the great Chinese Mystic and applied them to her own life. Soon she gained an astonishing control of her mind and her nerves. She changed so dramatically that her family hardly knew her. Her mind was more peaceful and calm at all times. She still had many problems of adjusting to her new life, especially in finding a new romantic partner, but she never again let herself become so reactive to her life situations that she could not control her moods and emotions.

ENJOY THE THINGS YOU NOW
HAVE RATHER THAN MAKE
YOURSELF MISERABLE LONGING
FOR THE UNATTAINABLE

6. Many people today are miserable because of the things they desire that they may never be able to have. We are in an age where living standards are very high and people can have color TV, home appliances that make housework easier, comfortable apartments and homes that are well-lighted and heated, a car to get to work or pleasure. These things are mostly taken for granted.

The people who are unhappy are those who want a bigger home, a more luxurious apartment, a more expensive car and two or three television sets. Many times, when these things are not available on a grand scale, they become miserable.

The way to handle this problem is to use and enjoy all the things you do have and not be unhappy because you do not have a big estate of your own, a mansion on Long Island, or a chauffeur-driven limousine. There is no harm in desiring these greater luxuries, but do not let that desire become a torment that keeps you from enjoying the comforts and benefits you now have.

LIVE IN THE PRESENT INSTEAD
OF PUTTING OFF LIVING TO
THE FUTURE

7. A Latin proverb says: "Dum vivimus, vivamus." Let us live while we live.

Confucius was a great believer in organizing your life in such a way that you can enjoy every single day fully and without regrets. Do the best you can for this one day only; be aware of the priceless privilege you have been given of having the gift of life. If you are healthy, sane and able to enjoy this moment, you should never worry about the future, nor think that you are being deprived of anything by life.

Testimony No. 37

Mr. & Mrs. N.H. Waited Too Long for Their Second Honeymoon

I knew a couple, Mr. and Mrs. N.H. who had worked hard all their lives to amass a fortune. They had never taken a trip abroad together. Their children had been reared and educated and they finally had a quarter of a million dollars invested in real estate in Los Angeles, California. This brought in a good income and people kept telling them they should let down a little and enjoy life. But Mr. H. kept saying, "No, we don't have enough money. When we have another $100,000 we'll take it easy and go on a second honeymoon around the world."

One day, they sold a piece of property that brought them the extra $100,000. "Now," Mr. N. said, "we can take that trip around the world." That day, he bought the tickets, returned home and told his wife they would begin their round the world trip on the following day. When his wife went to awaken him that morning, she found that he had died in his sleep!

Never put off living and enjoying yourself until you have a better job, or until you move to a better home, or until your children are grown up and on their own. That day may never come. Live for today and don't worry about tomorrow!

BUILD YOUR MENTAL GARDEN
WHERE OTHERS CAN SHARE YOUR
SIMPLE PLEASURES

8.   Many people are discontented because they are constantly searching in the outer world for pleasures and excitement. These people are on a constant round of external adventures, thinking they will find the elusive happiness for which they search. They frequent nightclubs, drink excessively, go on a constant round of cocktail parties and trips, thinking that by being busy they are ad-

ding to their life enjoyment.

Confucius taught that one must build his own mental garden where he can enjoy the simple pleasures of life with his family and friends. This idea was later adopted by the Grecian philosopher Epicurus. It is through the mind that we are able to experience life to the fullest and to enjoy living it. By building mental pleasures, things that are easy to satisfy, you can live a rich, full life and never feel lonely or deprived.

GOOD BOOKS, ART AND MUSIC
GIVE PLEASURE

Such mental pleasures consist in the appreciation of good books. A person who reads a great deal doubles and even triples his life experience. By sharing in the great thoughts and experiences of brilliant minds, you can expand the horizons of your own consciousness and have profound emotional experiences that enrich your life dramatically.

You can also build your mental garden with thoughts of great philosophers, like Confucius, Socrates, Plato and Aristotle, and weave into the fabric of your destiny some of the gold and silver threads that have illumined the tapestry of history.

Great music can also be an enriching emotional experience. Study the lives of the great composers, know their music, and revel in the magnificent harmonies their souls have revealed. You will find music of all ages and all cultures beneficial, for it is not only stimulating to your higher mind, but it is soothing and healing in times of stress and turbulence.

The art treasures of the world, paintings, sculpture and architecture can also be absorbed mentally to cushion you against the recurring shocks of ugliness and obscenity which we frequently find in modern life. You can obtain books which carry all of the world's great art treasures, and when your mind has been assaulted by the cacophony of ugliness to be found in much of everyday living, you can quietly retire into the inner garden of your mind and there absorb the highest standards of grandeur and beauty to be found in the world.

ENJOY THE BEAUTY IN NATURE
AND THE CHANGING SEASONS

9.   Confucius taught that man's soul must be attuned to natural beauty in the universe if it is to know peace and serenity. The great spiritual laws of the cosmos are all reflected in nature. When we study these phenomena through observing the miracles to be found in the world around us, we are better able to

attune our minds, hearts and souls to the natural rhythm of the universe and be in accord with the laws of balance, order and harmony. Emerson said:

Throb thine own with nature's throbbing breast, and all is clear from east to west.

LIVE IN THE WORLD OF
NATURAL SPLENDOR

Instead of seeking the artificial, man-made creations in the world that are subject to erosion and change, find your enjoyment by living a great deal in the world of natural splendor. Enjoy the forests, rivers and mountains. See the majesty of trees reaching up towards the celestial heights as though in perpetual prayer and adoration of the power that created them.

Be aware of the multitudes of flowers that carpet the earth with their perfumed glory. Never let a day pass without giving thanks to God for the panorama of beauty that he has spread like a verdant carpet for you to walk upon. See the mystical wonder of a full moon spreading its silvery rays over the distant ocean and the purple veil of night studded with billions of stars that share their mystery and wonder with earthlings. Be aware that you are riding on a carousel called Earth, spinning at dizzying speed around the golden sun, and that the divine laws holding this earth in space are the same ones that operate in your daily life to bring you health, happiness and fulfillment. Life is a mystical adventure and nature is the backdrop against which this great drama is being played out, so be aware of its infinite beauty and wonder during every day of your life.

PAVE YOUR PATHWAY TO
PARADISE WITH THE
GOLDEN DREAM
OF LOVE'S SWEET ECSTASY

10.   God has given man the divine emotion of love to help him cushion the shocks of daily realistic living. This golden dream has been placed within every human heart and soul. The reason it is so vitally important in finding the pathway to paradise is that Love is God's dream for His creation.

The poet Browning said:

Take away love and the earth is a tomb.

Every great achievement by man has been motivated by this divine emotion of love.

Try to find true love happiness early in life and let it be more precious to you than gold, silver or precious gems. To attract true love there must be a high ideal within your own heart and soul of this ennobling emotion. Today, many people have forgotten this concept of love, leading lives of permissiveness and promiscuity that shatter the sacredness of marriage and the home and the value of human life. We must once again build these ideals of spiritual love if civilization is to survive the recurring cataclysms of war and bloodshed and violence.

USE THE MYSTICAL LAW OF MENTAL ALCHEMY TO CHANGE THE NEGATIVE CONDITIONS OF LIFE INTO POSITIVE ONES

11.   The law of mental alchemy or transmutation is used by mystics to alter the chemistry of negative thinking and also to change the negative, unwanted and disastrous experiences of life into spiritual values.

When your mind sees evidences of perpetual disaster, disease, old age, war, death and destruction, the chemistry of your mind and body are alchemically altered into patterns that bring sickness and unhappiness.

HOW TO USE THE LAW OF MENTAL ALCHEMY TO CHANGE YOUR LIFE

Sit quietly in meditation and use the law of mental alchemy by stating:

I now change the negative conditions of my life into positive, happy, healthy ones.

I turn evil into good.

I become loving and forgiving and this dissolves hatred.

I see only peace and concord in my life and this banishes friction and discord.

I recognize the divinity in others and remove inharmony.

I see the world as being filled with treasures and this changes my powers of attraction from poverty to riches.

I recognize beauty all around me and this banishes ugliness.

I think healthy, happy and loving thoughts and this changes the chemistry of my body from acidity to alkalinity.

BUILD MENTAL AND SPIRITUAL VALUES AND RISE ABOVE THE MATERIALISTIC REALM TO FIND TRUE LASTING HAPPINESS

12.   The philosophy of materialism teaches that we must worship only physical and material things in this world. We make money our God; we live in the world of sensation and matter. We lose sight of the true, permanent, spiritual vaules that are behind life and upon which we must build if we wish to have lives of lasting and enduring success.

Mystic philosophy shows us the inner path to the finding of peace and contentment. Each day, go into quiet meditation and survey the events of your life. Ask yourself these questions:

- Am I really enjoying life?
- Do I build something of value each day that will endure?
- Have I put money and material things in their proper place?
- Am I living to give something of value to my family and to the world?
- Am I enriching my life by enriching my mind with the spiritual treasures that endure, such as art, literature, music, poetry and spiritual knowledge?
- Do I give daily thanks to God, the source of all my blessings?
- Do I express love daily to my family and my friends?
- Do I communicate with God through prayer and meditation, extolling daily His virtues and beneficence?

LAO-TSE'S PATHWAY TO HEAVEN

The poet and mystic Lao-Tse was one of Confucius' students and added another dimension to the great philosopher's teachings. He showed one that the pathway to heaven or Tao, could be easily achieved through the following method:

1.   Be gentle as a child and oppose no one, but yield gracefully. A child is appealing because it is harmless and everyone loves a child and wants to serve him. The master Jesus also said. "Except ye become as a little child ye shall not enter the kingdom of God."

2.   A falling drop of water will gradually carve the hardest rock, Lao-Tse taught. Water is the softest of all substances but its persistent action will remove the hardest rock gradually. So too we must use gentle language and actions to gradually wear away the obdurate, opposing forces of life, not force or violence.

3.   Live in the dream of love and the harsh experiences of life cannot harm you; hate destroys and greed erodes.

4.   Obey the cosmic laws of the universe and live under these moral, ethical, physical and spiritual laws taught by all the great Prophets and life will flow smoothly and easily.

5.   Attune your mind to the higher spiritual forces of the universe through daily prayer and meditation and you will receive divine guidance to help you overcome life's problems.

MYSTO-MATIC POINTERS

1. *Build your own mental and spiritual world, in which you can retire when misfortunes and tragedies strike. In this inner world, you will be fortified by the knowledge that all things are transient and that this too shall pass away.*

2. *Never try to hold onto anything or any person permanently. Everything is in a state of flux and new experiences can only come when we have released the old.*

3. *Curb your desires so that they do not get out of control. It is right to want the best that life has to offer, but do not let events make you unhappy if you cannot have everything you desire.*

4. *Enjoy all the good things of life and be happy in the knowledge that your destiny is already written in the stars and you cannot be too early or too late in coming into that ultimate destiny.*

5. *Adopt the inscrutable Oriental calm in which you do not register too much emotion at any time. Be peaceful in thought and present a personality of unruffled calm to the outer world.*

6. *Face both life and death with the knowledge that there is a divine plan to life and that death is a rebirth into another dimension of time and space in which the soul shall know its rewards.*

9

SECRETS OF ANCIENT YOGA FOR HEALTH, REJUVENATION AND LONG LIFE

The form of Indian Mysticism called Yoga deals with some of life's deepest mysteries and shows you how to control the forces back of life.

Yoga can be used to maintain the body's perfect health; it can also be used to rejuvenate the body and keep it functioning perfectly for one hundred years or more. But Yoga relates to more than the body, it shows how to gain mastery of the mind and the emotions, how to relax the body through meditation and exercise, and most important of all, Yoga reveals how you can attune your soul to the soul rhythm of the universe for mastery of life.

The word Yogi means the practitioner of the art of Yoga. Yoga, in ancient

Sanskrit means linked to or yoked to the power of the absolute, which we call God.

You will learn in this chapter how to use the mystical power of Yoga to elevate your consciousness to the higher realms of the absolute. This will give you unity and oneness with that cosmic mind which created the universe and which sustains all creation.

HOW TO RELEASE THE MYSTICAL POWER OF KUNDALINI FOR LIFE ENERGY

You will be shown how you can use the power of Yoga to control your mind and to direct the dynamic spirit of life within yourself. You will learn how to build powerful stores of nervous and emotional energy with which you can overcome mental and bodily fatigue, keeping your body forever healthy, strong and young. Through the release of the nervous energy known as Kundalini, you will learn how to use the stored-up reserves of magnetic and electrical energy that are held in reserve at the base of the spinal cord.

When you once discover how to release the mystical property or life force called Prana, you will have mental and spiritual elevation that can impel you to become a creative genius.

Your mind has a vast network of nerves that receive sensations from the outer world and your brain interprets these through touch, sight, sound, smell and taste. You can utilize this same system of nerve currents to send your mental impulses to others' minds, when they are sensitively attuned to the reception of these electrical pulsations. This system of mind communication is called extra sensory perception and includes the phenomena known as clairvoyance, clairaudience, telepathy, precognition, and psychic or intuitive guidance.

HOW TO ACHIEVE THE STATE OF HATHA YOGA FOR VITAL GOOD HEALTH

1.   The Sanskrit word *hatha* literally means "force." Hatha Yoga is concerned with the life force and the body. It can be used to perfect the power of your body and cause it to be healthy, vital and young.

The word Hatha is divided into two parts meaning the sun and the moon. The deep inhalations of breath are called sun breathing and the exhalations are termed moon breathing. These forms of deep inhalation strengthen the heart and other organs of the body as well as release the nerves and the brain from tension and daily stresses.

Through this form of Yoga the mind is called the Lord of the senses and the breath is called the Lord of the mind.

HOW TO ASSUME THE LOTUS
POSITION FOR MEDITATION

As you now prepare yourself for the state of meditation known as Hatha Yoga, seek out a comfortable place, where you can sit in the Lotus position if you care to. As you sit on the floor, you place the right foot on the left thigh and the left foot on the right thigh. You can do each of the seven stages of meditation one at a time, for only a few moments. Some prefer to do one of these meditations each day for seven days, taking longer to do them.

Now when you are in a comfortable position and relaxed, take a deep inhalation through the nostrils; hold it as long as you feel comfortable and then exhale slowly. As you inhale the breath, concentrate your mind on the golden rays of the sun. Mentally feel the sun's healing rays, sense its warmth spreading throughout your entire body.

As you exhale the breath, concentrate your mind on the full silvery moon, feeling its romance and mystery and sensing its peaceful, gentle presence throughout your body.

THE SACRED MANTRA—AUM
MANE PADME AUM—FOR
MEDITATION

As you close your eyes, you can intone the sacred mantra from Tibet, *Aum mane padme aum*, which means, "The jewel in the heart of the lotus."

You can then read the following Meditation, although later, when you acquire proficiency in the art of meditation, you can make up your own meditations:

> *I now meditate on control of the life force within my body. As the celestial fire flows throughout my brain and body it is healing me of all negative forces. I now control my thoughts, thinking only of the power of the golden sun that courses through my body with every healing breath. It is removing all impurities from my body and it heals me perfectly. I now control the nervous energy of my brain and body. It flows to every nerve of my body, giving me power to perform all life's functions perfectly. I now feel the surge of pranic*

*life force flowing through my nerves, and it overcomes all tensions
and stresses within my body. I become calm and poised. The reser-
voir of power within my higher mind centers is now released in a
floodtide of life energy, giving me strength, healing, youthful
vitality and the power to master life. Aum mane padme aum.*

THE SEVEN MYSTICAL CENTERS,
OR CHAKRAS, OF YOGA

In addition to the seven stages of Yoga for purposes of meditation, the
Ancients also taught that the release of Celestial Fire or Prana to the higher
levels of consciousness would bring about the opening of the mystical centers of
the brain and body that are known as *chakras.*

Each of the seven chakras is assigned to a definite locality in the body, and
when you meditate in each stage of Yoga, you will automatically concentrate on
each of the mystical chakras. As the Chakras open you will be given a new sense
of awareness of power for various purposes, depending on the location of that
particular Chakra.

HOW TO ACTIVATE THE SEVEN
CHAKRAS AND OPEN THE
PADMAS

As you now learn to activate these seven Chakras to high levels of action,
you will release a mystical force called the *padmas.* You will visualize a beautiful lotus flower of various colors. The subtle currents that are set up in your
higher mind centers will be very much like electricity that sets the wheels of a
machine into motion. When these higher mental and spiritual forces are
developed, you can perform seeming miracles that will astound others.

The first mystical chakra that you will open, while you are in the first stage
of Yoga known as Hatha Yoga, is called Muladhara, and the astral color for
concentration, is red. This Chakra is to be visualized as being at the base of your
spine.

Red is the symbol of the life force and the bloodstream that flows
throughout the body, healing it and giving it life energy. Four petals of the
Sacred Lotus are ascribed to this first Chakra.

Testimony No. 38

Desmond P. Overcame Illness and Depression Due to Age

Desmond P. was one of my students in California, who studied these mystical secrets of Yoga in our classes. When he came into the work he felt he no longer had a purpose in living. He was then sixty-five years of age and had already had many different forms of illness that kept him from being very active. He had already retired and was on social security. His wife had died, his children were on their own, and he told me that his life seemed barren and empty, without any purpose in living.

I recognized the symptoms that Desmond had, for he was listless, without energy or ambition, and he was taking all kinds of medications for a variety of illnesses. The first thing I had him do was to learn how to breathe deeply, as he had a slight cough and chest congestion that seemed to be the result of no special cause. I knew that the breath of life, when it is deeply inspired, must arouse the celestial spark within the brain, giving it a desire to live and to express life fully.

Desmond did the breathing exercises religiously, three times a day, breathing deeply, concentrating on the sun's golden rays, spreading throughout his brain and body. As he exhaled the breath, he concentrated on the full silvery moon, sensing its peace, magnetism and power flowing throughout his entire body. As he did his breathing he was told to concentrate on the base of his spine, where the first chakra is located, and see the pranic life force, like a red ball in a thermometer. As he breathed in slowly, he was to visualize that breath going down deep into the spinal column, stirring the life force at the base of the spine, and then as he breathed out, he was told that the red in the thermometer was rising slowly up his spinal column and being radiated to all parts of his body, his lungs, his heart, his stomach, his brain and all the vital organs.

This exercise in concentration helped Desmond open the first chakra, known as Muladhara, and released the celestial fire so it rose into his brain, flowed throughout his entire body, stimulating him and giving him the will to live and to become a creative human being once again.

After he had mastered the breathing techniques, Desmond repeated the above meditation that is given for opening the psychic centers through Hatha Yoga. In a few days, he had become more dynamic and vital. He suddenly had a purpose for living, and inspiration to achieve something in the future. His body functions improved, his vague aches and pains disappeared, and he told me that for the first time in years, he had hope and optimism for the future.

HOW TO ACHIEVE THE STATE OF
LAYA YOGA FOR QUIESCENCE

2.   The word *laya* literally means a concealed force within the body that is inactive and lambent. Scientists today call this power in the brain and body bio-plasmic energy. When your mind is quiescent and still, this lambent power flows naturally through the nerves and blood vessels to all parts of your brain and body, bringing about restoration of the life energy and perfect functioning of the body's organs.

However, in the state of Laya Yoga there is neither concentration nor projection of the mind in any direction. The mental force is held in a completely lambent state and the inner pranic force is used to awaken the power of Kundalini.

In this state of Laya Yoga you will learn how to concentrate on the second chakra, located at the juncture of the reproductive tract which is named Swadhishthana. You will visualize opening the six petals of the lotus, and ascribe the color reddish-orange.

MEDITATION FOR ACHIEVING
STATE OF LAYA YOGA

First, breathe deeply and achieve a state of quiescene by repeating the sacred *Aum mane padme aum* five times. Then, let your mind absorb the following meditation:

> *I now enter into the inner state of consciousness where there is peace and quiescence. I control my thoughts, so they reflect only joy and beauty and peace. I now control my nervous energy, so I am calm and poised. I now control my body, so it is responsive to my higher mind centers. I now project the pranic life force to the second chakra where it stirs up the creative fires of kundalini. I am now a channel for cosmic spirit to work its miracles through me. I am*

peaceful. I am powerful. I am poised. I am attuned to the soul of the universe. I am in the light and the light is all.

Testimony No. 39

How Deborah L. Used Laya Yoga to Achieve Inner Peace

Deborah L. was so highly nervous when she first came into our study of mysticism that she could not sit still through a class. She would fuss with her pocketbook, she would get up two or three times and go out into the hall to smoke a cigarette, and when she returned I could tell she was not really listening to the instructions I was giving.

When I had my first consultation with Deborah she told me that her marriage had already broken up. She said this was due to irritability and impatience. She found fault with her husband, she accused him of infidelity, and she had the feeling that something tragic was about to happen. Of course, this mental attitude did cause her husband to finally leave her, and then she became so neurotic that she could not sleep nights, began taking sleeping pills and then tranquilizers, until she was finally so nervous that she could no longer work and had to go on welfare.

In our second consultation, I began to work with Laya Yoga meditations and concentration so that Deborah could control her mind and her nerves. As she had a cigarette and sleeping pill habit to overcome, it was more difficult and took somewhat longer for her to begin to have results. In one month, she had reduced her cigarette smoking to five a day; she was no longer on sleeping pills, for she found she could go to sleep almost instantly after saying the Laya Yoga meditation several times.

SEXUAL DIFFICULTIES CAN BE OVERCOME THROUGH USE OF YOGA EXERCISES

She had told me that part of her difficulty was that she had no emotional response to her husband sexually. She found her mind drifting and she was totally unresponsive, until the sexual act became so obnoxious that she actually felt ill each time her husband made demands of her.

To help her overcome this problem of frigidity and lack of sexual response, I gave her the concentration on the second chakra, Swadhishthana, at the juncture of the genitals, and told her to visualize opening the six petals in that area, visualizing the astral color of reddish-orange.

MEDITATION TO HELP
OVERCOME THE PROBLEM OF
FRIGIDITY IN SEX

She was to use the following meditation statement for that purpose.

I now project the pranic life force to the creative and reproductive centers of my being. I feel the flow of cosmic energy that gives me life. I am now aware of the lambent procreative power that dwells within me. I now attune my mind and body to the creative power of divine love. I release this creative power to every cell of my brain and body and I am healed of all malfunctioning. I now concentrate on opening the six petals of the lotus, flooded with the astral colors of orange and red. The petal of peace now opens and reveals an inner world of infinite peace. The petal of Beauty, now reveals a world of infinite beauty. The petal of joy now reveals that I am surrounded by infinite joy. The petal of Love reveals God's own loving spirit which now animates my brain, body and soul with this divine emotion. The petal of Good now opens, flooding my life with good. The petal of hope now opens, bringing me the promise of eternal bliss and joyous fulfillment of my life dream.

I am happy to report that within a period of two months, Deborah was able to achieve a complete healing. She used all the other forms of meditation we shall study, and was soon able to attract her true soul mate and find marital bliss and fulfillment. Better still, her smoking and pill habit were completely conquered and she began to have more energy and vitality than ever before. She went back to her work as a legal secretary and her life suddenly became beautiful.

HOW TO ACHIEVE THE STATE OF
MANTRA YOGA FOR PSYCHIC
POWER

3. Before going into any state of meditation you will always recite a mantra, which is a poetic or spiritual word or phrase which brings about psychological and physiological changes in the mind and body.

You can recite these sacred and ritualistic mantras while you hold your mind in absolute concentration on the purpose for which you are saying the mantra. In the forms of Mantra Yoga that we shall now study, you will be opening the psychic third eye to achieve psychic power, including clairvoyance, clairaudience, precognition and divine intuition.

MEDITATION FOR ACHIEVING
THE STATE OF MANTRA YOGA

As you sit in meditation, you can adopt the lotus position, but be sure that you are relaxed mentally and physically. The sacred word AUM, pronounced OHM, will be used for this particular meditation, although you can recite other words and phrases later, to achieve definite effects. For instance, the words peace, love, joy, beauty, good, can also be used for one-word Mantras to achieve the qualities designated by the words. While you do this Mantra Meditation you will concentrate your mental force on the third chakra, which is located near the navel, and which ranges in color from green to gold. There are twelve petals ascribed to this particular chakra. This third chakra is called Manipura.

Now say the sacred mantra *Aum* ten to fifteen times, with the lips closed. Let the vibration of the *Aum* linger on the lips and the mask of the face. As this hum rises to the head area it will stimulate your higher psychic centers, giving you insight, perception and divine intuition.

Now read the following meditation statement:

I now withdraw my sense perceptions from the outer world of reality and enter into the world of dreams. I now contact the cosmic mind which created me and knows all the secrets of the universe. I stimulate the psychic third eye and achieve psychic perception. I ask that the veil be pulled aside so I may view the future destiny that I shall attain. I now ask for the gifts of clairvoyance and clairaudience. I attune my higher psychic mind centers to the cosmic mind of God and I am now one with the power that knows all, sees all and is all.

HOW TO ACHIEVE THE STATE OF
BHAKTI YOGA FOR SPIRITUAL
ECSTASY

4.   The form of Bhakti Yoga which inspires spiritual ecstasy is that which is used most widely in India today. This can be combined with Mantra Yoga, or with the other forms of Yoga given here if you wish to do all seven stages of meditation on any one day.

Through Bhakti Yoga you can achieve a merging with the Absolute and know the transcendental joy that comes when you are able to rise above the world of matter into the illimitable stratosphere of absolute power, absolute intelligence, absolute good, absolute beauty, absolute peace, absolute joy and absolute love.

MEDITATION FOR ACHIEVING THE STATE OF BHAKTI YOGA FOR SPIRITUAL ECSTASY

Sit in quiet meditation and concentrate your mental force on the fourth chakra known as the Heart Wheel, which is located in the region of the heart.

This chakra is called Anahata and you will visualize twelve golden leaves of the lotus, merging towards the color red.

After you have said the sacred Mantra from Tibet, *Aum mane padme aum,* ten times, you will read the following meditation statement:

I now control my mind and my body, so I am in perfect stillness. I ascend the spiritual mountaintop and rise above the gravity pull of mind, body and emotions. As I ascend into the lofty stratosphere of pure divine essence I blend with the Absolute. I now experience the transcendental feeling of divine love. My soul now blends with the soul of the universe in the divine romance that shall last throughout eternity. I now experience absolute power. Absolute knowledge and wisdom are now mine to know all secrets of the universe. I experience absolute good in all my relationships with others. I wear the divine mantle of absolute peace and tranquility. I live in an aura of absolute beauty that makes all of life a scintillating adventure. I express absolute love to everyone I meet. I am now in the light and the light is all.

BHAKTI YOGA CAN BE USED TO HEAL HEART CONDITIONS

This Bhakti Yoga meditation may be used by anyone who wishes a spiritual healing of some bodily ailment, as well as for purposes of devotion and spiritual ecstasy. It has been found that the concentration on the Heart Wheel, which is the fourth chakra, will actually stimulate that organ, causing it to direct healing currents to various parts of the body. When there is peace and tranquility in the mind, the body is automatically on the way to being healed.

Testimony No. 40

Douglas J. Used Bhakti Yoga to Heal a Heart Condition

Douglas J. was an instance of such a dramatic healing of a heart condition. In his case he had already had two heart attacks. He had recovered each time but was weak and nearly immobilized. He came into our study of Mysticism and learned how to go into the various stages of Yoga, especially concentrating on the form known as Bhakti Yoga and the fourth chakra, the Heart Wheel.

After doing the above meditation to achieve absolute power, peace and poise, he then concentrated his mental force on the Heart Wheel, talking directly to his heart with the following meditation statement. As he did this meditation he closed his fist and opened it, stimulating the action of his heart throughout the meditation. when your hand is closed it is about the size of the human heart. He then said this meditation:

YOGA MEDITATION FOR
HEALING A HEART CONDITION

I now direct the life force to my beating heart. As I open and close my hand, to the count of seventy-two beats per minute, my heart will be stimulated and directed to maintain that cosmic rhythm of life. Cosmic life energy now flows from my higher psychic mind centers to my beating heart. I am in tune with the universal life rhythm that decrees I shall live for one hundred years or more. My heart is now being healed of all malfunctioning. I am peaceful and still. This peace and stillness now extends to my heart causing it to function perfectly. I am life. I am energy. I am creative intelligence. I am one with the cosmic power that created me and which now sustains me in perfect health.

HOW TO ACHIEVE THE STATE OF
KARMA YOGA FOR MENTAL,
PHYSICAL AND SPIRITUAL
BALANCE

5.　Karma Yoga deals with physical and bodily action. The word is derived from the Sanskrit and means to do, or the law of action and reaction, cause and effect.

Karma Yoga is also known as the universal law of justice or compensation. Karma is a two-edged sword; it can punish us when we violate the moral, ethical, physical or spiritual laws, and it can reward us, when we live under the laws of the cosmos.

Karma is tied in with the belief in reincarnation among three quarters of the people on the face of the earth. They believe that we build up merits or demerits in this life or in past lives and that the purpose in living is to overcome this negative karma and transmute it into positive or good karma.

In practicing Karma Yoga you will attempt to overcome the negative forces that create bad karma and enthrone the good forces that create positive karma. The negative karmic forces are: fear, worry, hate, greed, selfishness, envy, jealousy and revenge. The good karmic forces are: honesty, justice, good, peace, truth, charity, love, and worship.

MEDITATION FOR ACHIEVING
KARMA YOGA FOR BALANCE

After intoning the sacred mantra *Aum Mane padme aum* four or five times you can read the following meditation statement:

> *I am now aware of the dynamic law of karma that operates in my mental, physical and spiritual life. I overcome the demerits that my soul has built through negative thoughts, actions and emotions. I now substitute only positive thoughts and actions for these demerits. I live under the cosmic law of truth and my life reflects honesty and goodness. I do only good for others and thus banish the karmic force of evil. I live under the spiritual laws of justice, love and forgiveness and achieve my true spiritual karmic destiny. My mental actions are positive and only positive results can occur in my body and my environment.*

When you practice Karma Yoga you can combine this with concentration on the fifth chakra called Vishuddha, which is located at the base of the throat. This chakra is imagined as having sixteen lotus petals. These petals are to be visualized as being a fiery gold or vivid lilac.

HOW TO ACHIEVE THE STATE OF
JNANA YOGA FOR SPIRITUAL
GROWTH

6.   The word Jnana literally means "to know." By using Jnana Yoga the searcher for truth evolves and grows spiritually by absorbing knowledge in this mystical journey through life.

You can begin the practice of Jnana Yoga with this statement of fact: "The Absolute is."

Then, as you go into meditation you can ask your higher mind specific questions relating to this Absolute power behind life, such as:

- Why was I born into this existence?
- What is the purpose behind my life?
- What is the soul?
- Who is God?
- What is my karmic destiny?

This type of self-probing and questioning draws from the infinite the ultimate truth as to the nature of God, of man, of the soul and of the true purpose behind life.

MEDITATION FOR ACHIEVING THE STATE OF JNANA YOGA

I now enter into meditation to search for the ultimate answer to the mystery behind life. The Absolute Is and no other power can negate or change this basic fact. I am Divine, created in the image and likeness of God. I possess all of the divine potentials within my own immortal soul. I express divinity in my thoughts, words and actions. God is love. I now reflect His loving presence in my inner and outer personality. God is good. I now reflect that goodness in my words and deeds. God is Infinite spirit and that spirit now animates me with the expression of life, peace, joy, good, beauty and love. The Absolute IS, and I am one with the Absolute expressing universal Truth and good.

HOW TO ACTIVATE THE SIXTH CHAKRA FOR SPIRITUAL POWER

When you do the Jnana Yoga meditation you will concentrate your mental force on the sixth chakra, which is located between the eyes on the level of the eyebrows. It is named Ajna, and the two petals of the lotus comprising this symbol are visualized as being the sun and the moon. It is here that the two pranic currents from the spine cross each other. The current on the right is known as Pingala, and on the left as Ida. Visualize the astral color of rose, and ascribe two petals of the lotus to this Chakra.

As it is in this area of the head that the third eye is located, you can use this as a focal point of concentration when you wish to open the third eye to achieve psychic vision.

HOW TO ACHIEVE THE STATE OF
RAJAH OR ROYAL YOGA FOR
UNFOLDING THE INNER SELF AND
ATTAINING NIRVANA

7.   It is through the Rajah branch of Yoga that you can achieve the unfolding of the inner self, the mastery of the mind, the nerves and the emotions
and attain that final last state of exaltation called blending with the soul of the
universe, or finding Nirvana. Sometimes this state of Yoga is known as passing
through the Golden Gate of Brahma. It is in this last stage of Yoga that you can
achieve complete Mastership.

The word Rajah signifies king; that is why this branch of Yoga is often
called Royal Yoga. This stage of Yoga deals with the highest intellectual
achievements and the development of the spiritual faculties in man. The body
cannot exist without the mind and the mind cannot exist without the spirit. This
spirit relates to the Infinite Mind of God, which in mysticism is often called the
Cosmic Mind.

Through Rajah Yoga you will concentrate the powers of your mind and
spirit on the spiritual reality of the higher self, or the nature of God, which is
called the Absolute.

HOW TO USE RAJAH YOGA TO
ELEVATE YOUR CONSCIOUSNESS
TO HIGH INSPIRATION

Through Rajah or Royal Yoga you will remove the mind-consciousness
from thoughts about your body or the emotions. You will still your conscious
mind with its fears and anxieties and petty problems. You will then be able to
elevate your consciousness to the lofty realms of great inspiration, worship and
devotion, dedication and divine love. Then, and only then will you be able to
find that realm of infinite peace and joy in which you will know soul harmony
and blend with the soul of the universe. In this state of consciousness that is
beyond good or evil, you will find nirvana, that blissful state where there is no
pain, no old age and no death—but only the glorious dream of life, love, immortality and soul union with the soul of the universe in the divine romance that
lasts throughout eternity.

MEDITATION FOR ACHIEVING
RAJAH YOGA

I now enter into the state of meditation where I shall achieve complete control of my mind, my emotions and my nerves. I rise above problems of earth and body sensations. I enter into the realm of the absolute, where I discover the realm of the supersensible. I am now inspired with the awareness of my true soul's identity. I reflect the golden glory of the cosmic spirit of God. I dedicate my life to serving God and humanity. I enshrine the noble emotion of love and devotion. I blend with the absolute and know eternal bliss and peace. I now enter through the sacred golden door of Brahma into the celestial realm of eternal light, where I take on the raiment of my soul's immortality and I become one with the Light.

THE SEVENTH CHAKRA TO USE
WITH RAJAH AND ROYAL YOGA

The seventh Chakra is represented as Sahasrara, and is the highest realm of concentration. This is the Chakra that is in the Crown or the very top of the head.

This seventh Chakra is to be visualized as the thousand and one petals of the Lotus and is every combination of colors. In mysticism Sahasrara is considered as being infinite expansion, it permeates all time and space and cannot be confined to the mind or body.

As you meditate on this seventh Chakra you can mentally repeat what follows:

I now concentrate all powers on the Infinite realm that represents the absolute. I am now yoked to this infinite power and experience infinite good. My brain and body are now attuned to the highest spiritual forces of the universe and I am in the light of His infinite peace, beauty, goodness, and love.

MYSTO-MATIC POINTERS

1. *To maintain the body in good health, the Yogi practices a rigid diet. He eats no red-blooded meat, he eats mostly grains, vegetables, fruits and what could be called a*

lacto-vegetarian diet. He avoids coffee, tea, alcohol, tobacco and drugs.

2. Make a point to practice one of the seven forms of Yoga each day for at least half an hour.

3. Be aware of your breathing several times a day; stop what you are doing and consciously breathe ten or fifteen times, giving your body a chance to replace the toxic poisons with fresh oxygen.

4. When you concentrate on each of the seven chakras you can do so for a few moments each, visualizing the area of the body in which the chakra is located and sending your Pranic Life force to that area to stimulate it and heal it.

5. To use Mantra Yoga each day make it a point to use a certain Mantra when you go into meditation. This can be the simple AUM, repeated ten times, or the entire mantra aum mane padme aum.

6. To achieve peace and tranquility you can sit in meditation and visualize the grandeur of a mountaintop. By holding your mind on this mountain peak, you will rise above the world of problems and worries.

7. In opening the petals of the Sacred Lotus, give each quality a color and meditate on that color as the petals open. You can use a new petal each day, such as for peace, love, joy, good, prosperity, health.

10

REINCARNATION—PINPOINT YOUR DESTINY ON THE KARMIC WHEEL OF FATE

More than two-thirds of the people on the face of the earth believe in Reincarnation. At one time the whole civilized world believed in the soul's return to this earth in another body, after the transition known as death.

Metempsychosis, as reincarnation is called, believes that man's soul must continue to be born, to live, to grow old and to die, as long as the soul fails to learn the lessons that would assure its passage into the realms of immortality or Nirvana. This coincides with the Christian belief that man's soul will be rewarded for good deeds in a paradise that is known as Heaven, and that his soul will be punished for evil deeds, in a region known as hell.

Instead of using the terms heaven and hell the ancients named it Nirvana and Karma. A person's good deeds build credits or merits in the book of life, which is called Karma. This good Karma rewards a person in each successive lifetime until he has paid all his demerits or bad Karma for evil acts that have been committed in past lives. Then the soul is released from the necessity of being born again in a physical body and ascends to its heavenly rewards, to live perpetually in the Golden Presence of God, in Nirvana.

REINCARNATION ACCOUNTS FOR LIFE'S CRUEL INEQUITIES

Why is it that seemingly innocent children are born blind, deaf, crippled and deformed? In reincarnation it is believed that these unfortunate souls need to learn important spiritual lessons that will free them from the Karmic wheel of fate.

Why are some people born into the Rockefeller or Onassis families and have ready-made wealth and power given to them when born, while others are born poor, underprivileged and deprived? Reincarnation teaches that the soul at birth seeks out parents that will give the soul a unique opportunity to work out its Karmic fate according to its needs.

In this way, each soul is given an equal opportunity, over successive lifetimes, to overcome misfortunes and tragedy and to build the destiny that is ultimately reserved for those who live under the great spiritual laws that govern the universe.

THE BENEFITS THAT YOU CAN DERIVE FROM A KNOWLEDGE OF REINCARNATION

Before giving you the benefits that may be derived from a knowledge of the laws of reincarnation, it is important that you understand a little of the history of this great mystical law of reincarnation.

In the Middle East and Far East, the ancient Arabian and Mohammedan writers taught their followers reincarnation as a reality. Caesar discovered the belief among the ancient Gauls, and reincarnation was believed in by the Gauls, the Celts and Britons in their earliest religious ceremonies.

This ancient belief of reincarnation was found in Peru and Mexico. It is to be found also in the Kabalistic rites of the ancient Hebrews. To the Jews it was believed that John the Baptist was a second Elijah. Even Jesus, after His resurrection, was believed to be John the Baptist or one of the old prophets, returned to earth in a different body.

Quite a respectable group of philosophers and geniuses in all fields had a deep belief in reincarnation, including Kant, Schelling, Leibnitz, Schopenhauer, Bruno, Herder, Lessing and Goethe. They all believed that the soul would return to earth in another form.

Scientists Flamarion, Figuier and Brewster also subscribed to this ancient belief of reincarnation. The noted theological leaders of past days also believed in this phenomenon. Some of them were Muller, Dorner, Ernesti, Edward Beecher, Bohme, Swedenborg, and in more recent times, Ralph Waldo Emerson, the American Transcendental philosopher.

Two-thirds of the human race today believes that the soul will return to earth in another body after death. This includes the Burmans, the Chinese, Japanese, Tartars, Tibetans, and East Indians. In Egypt reincarnation was part of the ancient rites in the Temples of Isis and Osiris.

Anything with such wide-spread belief deserves our philosophical investigation.

REINCARNATION HELPS YOU
BETTER UNDERSTAND THE
MYSTERIES OF LIFE

As a spiritual belief, reincarnation will help you understand many of the mysteries of life. It will give you a sane and sensible explanation for the many misfortunes and tragedies which occur to innocent people for which we can give no rational explanation. Why do thousands of young men have to die on fields of battle without ever having a chance to work out their destinies on this earth? Reincarnation explains that they will have another chance in another lifetime. Their misfortunes were due to some sins committed in past lives, for which they are atoning in this life.

You can learn how to work out your own life Karma in this one lifetime, so you need not suffer from mistakes that you committed in past lifetimes. You can build merits while still in this body, so when your soul makes its transition, it can rise a step higher in the spiritual evolutionary ladder of destiny, and reach new heights of achievement.

Geniuses like Leonardo da Vinci, Michelangelo, Shakespeare, Columbus, Beethoven, Byron, Socrates, Edison and Lincoln, could never have risen to their magnificent heights in one single lifetime. This is the argument that reincarnationists use to explain why some people are born geniuses while others never develop their full potentials in one lifetime.

HOW YOU CAN KNOW YOUR
PAST LIVES AND YOUR KARMA

It is possible for you to know your past lives and then learn to work out your Karmic Destiny in this lifetime, so you can avoid many of life's tragic experiences and much of its suffering.

If you are attracted to a certain period of history very strongly and read and study everything you can about that era then you undoubtedly have a strong karmic affinity for that time and you may have lived a lifetime in that cycle.

Testimony No. 41

Proof That He Had Lived in Another Lifetime

A man named Richard T. had a very strong feeling that he had lived in the French courts before the revolution. He had a strong desire to read everything he could find about the history of France. Although he was not French in this lifetime, he had an instant feeling for the French language and after a short study, he found himself proficient in the language. He had recurring psychic dreams in which he saw himself involved in the pomp and ceremony of the French courts. In one vivid dream he found himself at the head of troops as a General and he was killed in battle. When he awakened from this Astral projection, for it was more than a dream, he wrote down all the details he could remember and later he looked up that historic battle and found that a certain General had indeed been killed in that war!

When he visited Paris, France, and went to Versailles, he immediately knew his way around the palace, and as he stood in the great mirrored halls, he knew that he had been there before.

SIGNS THAT CAN REVEAL YOUR
PAST INCARNATIONS

Here are some of the signs you can look for that could guide you to a knowledge of former lives:

1.   If you persistently have vivid astral dreams of foreign places or historic events, in which you seem to be an active participant, then it is likely that these are left-over memories of past incarnations. For instance, you may

have a recurring astral dream that you are in India, walking besides the Ganges, or in some ancient temple participating in religious ceremonies. Or you may find yourself in ancient Egypt, involved in some mystical experiences in the King's Chamber in the vast Pyramid of Cheops. You will have vivid recollections of the ceremonies being performed and you may find yourself instinctively knowing certain things about Egypt and the Pyramids, or the tombs of the ancient Pharoahs that are later borne out by actual excavations and discoveries.

Testimony No. 42

An Astral Dream Revealed to Laura G. She Had Lived in Ancient Egypt

A member of our California lecture group Laura G. had such a vivid Astral dream that she accurately drew pictures of the King's chamber in the great pyramid of Giza, and told the class details about her experiences in that ancient land. When we went there as a group some months later, she compared her drawings of her astral revelations with the actual King's chamber and all details were exactly as she had described them!

2. You may be very strongly attracted to a branch of art that relates to some historical period, such as ancient Chinese art or Grecian sculpture, or art of some other period in history. If you study all the known revelations about that period and have the persistent feeling that you have known these things in another lifetime, then perhaps this is a flashback to your period of reincarnation to that era and it is being relived in your astral dreams.

Testimony No. 43

Linda C. Had Astral Proof of a Chinese Reincarnation

Linda C. was such a person, who told me in our classes in mysticism, that she loved everything about ancient Chinese art. She collected miniature vases of that period of history, she had finely embroidered materials that depicted Chinese objects. She knew the drama, poetry and literature of the various periods of Chinese history. She often had vivid astral dreams in which she saw herself in an ancient Chinese palace, sitting on a throne, and being a powerful Empress. One vivid dream ended that royal epoch, for she dreamed that invading hordes from the north, swept into the palace and murdered her. After that time she never again had the same astral dream.

When Linda G. was regressed in hypnotic sleep back to her past lives, she accurately recalled the entire scene and spoke a form of ancient Chinese that has not been used for centuries!

REPETITION OF LIFE
EXPERIENCES, PROOF OF PAST
LIVES AND KARMA

3.   If you keep attracting one life experience over and over again and it brings you suffering and pain, you may be re-living a past karmic period in your reincarnations that is intended to give you a spiritual lesson. If you overcome that karma by instinctively doing things that help you lessen it, you will be freed from the painful experience.

For instance, some people marry a person who is obviously unsuited to them; they divorce and then marry again, and this often continues five or six times, without the person ever learning the karmic lesson involved. This form of karma indicates that in past lives the person may have been cruel or selfish or in some way unfit for the marriage state. The same marital tragedies will continue until the person has learned how to work out that karma and rise above the recurring situation in marriage.

If you find yourself facing any life situation that never seems to change and it is one of frustration, poverty, unhappiness, lack of love fulfillment or any other distressing life problem, then your inability to rise above it may be tied in with your karmic necessity to work out some problem connected with past lives. If you once learn how to master that karma, you can then end the period of suffering and privation and know the freedom and joy that come when you pay your karmic debts in this lifetime.

PLAYBACK OF SOME PAST EVENT
COULD BE PROOF OF
REINCARNATION

4.   If you are in some life situation that you feel has occurred before, exactly as it unfolds before your eyes, then it could be a replay of some past lifetime

period where a similar situation took place. For instance, you may suddenly enter a room where you feel you have been before; you suddenly know that a person is going to be there, that the person will say something that is familiar, or that you will hear music playing at that moment, all these things flash across your consciousness vividly and are then played out accurately. You will know then that you are reliving a dimension of time that accurately shadows some past life experience in another reincarnation.

GENIUSES OFTEN ACQUIRED
BRILLIANCY IN PAST LIVES

5.   Some people who have proofs that they have lived before are those who are born with a mathematical capacity for instantly being able to add, multiply or subtract rows of figures entirely in their heads. One such young child was able to do these astounding feats in mathematics with great ease and no tutoring. He could have carried this amazing ability over from another incarnation.

Still others have a capacity for musical composition, or poetry or writing stories, by simply sitting down and letting themselves be used as channels for the creative work that was undoubtedly learned in former incarnations.

Great inventors have often been thought to be incarnations of advanced souls like Leonardo da Vinci, Copernicus, Galileo or other geniuses who have lived in the past. Certainly some explanation is possible when great souls like Einstein, Edison, Lincoln, and Columbus, are able to advance the cause of science, exploration, political history and invention as they did. They and millions of other gifted souls must have acquired their skills and brilliance in other lifetimes.

HOW TO READ THE AKASHIC
RECORD OF PAST
REINCARNATIONS ON ASTRAL
PLANES

6.   You can ask your soul to release information about your Akashic record when you go to sleep at night and go out on an astral journey. The Akashic record is the history of your past lives and it is carried by your soul through each successive lifetime.

Just before you go to sleep at night, instruct your soul to go out onto the astral planes, as given in another chapter in this book, and tell your soul you wish to visit the eras in history where you have lived before and remember these periods of past lives. Then, when you awaken from your astral projection, jot down the details of the vivid astral dreams you had. These will often be the reincarnations that you have had in former times.

HOW YOU CAN WORK OUT YOUR KARMIC DESTINY IN THIS LIFETIME

It is very often possible that a person can pay his karmic debts in this lifetime. If you find yourself having recurring periods of misfortune, sickness, poverty, unhappiness or tragedy, you will know that these are karmic demerits that have been built up by your soul in past lifetimes. Here is the regimen for wiping out these karmic demerits in this lifetime and then being able to enjoy your life from that time on.

1.   You can lessen your karmic debts by living under the spiritual laws of the universe. These are in the Ten Commandments, the Golden Rule and the Sermon on the Mount. They are also given in the spiritual revelations of all the great Prophets of history.

2.   You can begin to live under a moral code of honesty, goodness, unselfishness, kindness and forgiveness. If someone hurts you, forgive that person and respond with love rather than hate. The Master Jesus spoke of it as "turning the other cheek." This is symbolic of course, and means that you avoid retaliation, performing an opposite act of love and kindness instead.

3.   You should try to be charitable towards others; helping those who are less fortunate, uplifting the lowly, educating the ignorant, giving love to those who need it, and trying to dispel the ignorance, superstition, war and poverty that bring so much karmic suffering to humanity.

4.   You can practice the divine emotion of love towards all God's creatures, hating no one, but only hating the evil that exists in the world. In this way, you will avoid the karmic demerits that hate often brings.

5.   You will begin to forgive others who commit wrongdoing against you, not wishing to harm them or have revenge against them. Feelings of revenge only build your emotions of hate and violence, causing you to commit acts that add to your karmic debts, causing you suffering, sickness and misery.

6.   You will have daily periods of prayer and meditation in which your soul will be attuned to the soul of the universe. These meditations will help purify your mind and spirit, giving you the ability to contact the cosmic mind

that can guide you through your higher psychic centers to a life that is free of karmic debts of pain, sickness, suffering, animalism and hate.

THE ACTS THAT INCREASE YOUR
KARMIC DEBT

You are increasing your karmic debt:

1.   When you are immersed in the self to the exclusion of all others and indulge your ego through boastfulness, egotism and acts that demean or degrade others.

2.   By taking actions that are cruel, inconsiderate and unkind.

3.   By practicing immoderation and polluting the body with foods and drinks that are harmful. This includes smoking, drinking alcohol excessively and eating foods that are harmful to the body. It also includes uncontrolled sexual appetites or descending to the level of animalism in promiscuity and immorality.

4.   By being obscene, coarse, common and vulgar. Also by indulging the temper and losing control of oneself and doing acts that are violent and harmful to others.

5.   By being combative and bad tempered most of the time, never letting others have peace of mind or emotional security.

6.   By letting the uncontrolled desire for power, fame or fortune unbalance the mind, causing one to commit acts of ruthlessness and aggression against the world. We see such karmic acts in the history of the world, Napoleon, Mussolini, Hitler, the Shah of Iran, (who lost his throne because of alleged acts of cruelty) and many others who have brought about war, insurrection and violence in history.

When you once learn how to use the lessons of past reincarnations in a positive way, you can rise above the gravity pull of earth into the spiritual stratosphere where goodness, love, truth, peace, charity and virtue abide, bringing one into the perfect state of bliss which the ancients called Nirvana.

MYSTO-MATIC POINTERS

1. If it is revealed to you that you have Karmic demerits from mistakes made in former incarnations, you can set to work in this life to correct these. An alcoholic or dope addict might review his life and decide that he must cor-

rect this negative karma. A person who suffers from poverty can decide that his Karma will be changed to one of success and riches.

2. If you have some Karma that seems to doom you to a life that is limited in some way, such as being blind, crippled, or incapacitated, try to bear your suffering with spiritual poise, thus helping erase the negative karma in this lifetime.

3. If other people constantly abuse you, this may be caused by past Karma in which you were abusive to others. Try to stand the abuse but change your mental attitude towards life and treat others kindly and with forgiveness.

4. Study the spiritual teachings of past mystics and prophets so you can acquire all the knowledge you need to help overcome Karma.

5. Obey the Karmic laws for honesty, justice, tolerence, good, forgiveness, charity and love, and you will lessen your own suffering.

6. If your love life or marriage is unhappy, try to correct this Karma from other reincarnations by changing your character and being more loving, forgiving and tolerant in your romantic life or marriage.

11

UNLOCKING THE SECRETS OF YIN-YANG FROM ANCIENT CHINA FOR A MAGNETIC LIFE OF POWER AND RICHES

In the mystical revelations from ancient China known as the Yin-Yang forces that are behind the universe, it was found that there are two polarities in life: One, the positive force known as Yang and the other, the negative force known as Yin.

You will now learn how to channel these two forces of Yin and Yang into your own life, receiving benefits from both, so you can achieve a balanced state of existence that can give you a magnetic life of power, riches and abundance.

THE FORCE OF COSMIC
MAGNETISM KNOWN TO THE
ANCIENT CHINESE

Centuries before modern scientists discovered the cosmic law of magnetism, the Ancient Chinese knew that there was a magnetic, invisible force in the universe that sustained all creation and which kept the planets spinning in space.

Magnetism has two polarities, one positive, the other negative. The Yin force is the negative polarity of magnetism, and the Yang force is the positive polarity. Both are essential to the proper functioning of the visible and the invisible universe.

Emerson, who was a great student of Oriental Mysticism and Indian Philosophy, stated, "All nature is bisected by a duality."

When there is a perfect balance between the Yin and Yang forces of the mind, there will be sanity, peace and tranquility.

This magnetic balance within your body between the forces of Yin and Yang will bring you perfect health and a long life.

A knowledge of which foods are Yin and which are Yang, and their effects upon your body, will help you determine your diet for life, giving you perfect balance, helping you overcome a weight problem and establishing a necessary balance between alkaline foods and acid foods.

A study of the Yin-Yang qualities in your personality will help you overcome self-consciousness, inferiority, inadequacy and personality defects that might doom you to social and business failure.

THE TWO FORCES OF MAGNETISM
IN YIN-YANG WHICH OPPOSE
EACH OTHER

POSITIVE: yang forces	NEGATIVE: yin forces
GOOD	EVIL
LOVE	HATE
RICHES	POVERTY
HEALTH	SICKNESS

PEACE	WAR
LIGHT	DARKNESS
INTELLIGENCE	IGNORANCE
YOUTH	AGE
BEAUTY	UGLINESS
HUMAN	ANIMAL
LIFE	DEATH
STRENGTH	WEAKNESS
HAPPINESS	MISERY
HEAVEN	HELL
GOD	DEVIL

Now you will be shown how to apply this magnetic principle of Yin-Yang to your own life. If you find that you are operating too much under the influence of Yin, which is the negative polarity of magnetism, you can immediately change your polarity of magnetic attraction to the positive side, and you will see instant, dramatic changes in your personality and your life experiences.

WHAT HAPPENS IF YOUR PERSONALITY HAS TOO MUCH OF THE YIN FORCE

If your personality has too much yin, you will be unmagnetic, and you will do the following things:

1. You will drift through life, giving in to the wishes of others and making no demands on others for your share of happiness, riches, love and fulfillment.
2. You will give up easily when faced with challenges and obstacles that stand in your path of destiny.
3. You are apt to be self-conscious, inferior and have feelings of inadequacy in most of your life situations.

4. You will withdraw in confusion and fear when challenged by people or difficult life situations.

5. You are apt to follow others, even when they might be wrong. You will rarely be a leader in any life situations. (See how this Yin quality dominated the thinking of Nazi Germany during the reign of Hitler! Germany normally is a Yang nation, with qualities of aggression and dominance, but through mass hypnosis, Hitler changed them into the Yin qualities of submissiveness and helplessness.)

6. You will see only the dark side of life and be filled with fear, worry and anxiety. This pessimism kills magnetism.

7. You will act from emotional impulsiveness to every life situation rather than from rationality and reason.

8. You will be inclined to accept the destiny into which you were born and make little or no effort to change things.

BUILD THE YANG FORCE OF
MAGNETISM IN YOUR
PERSONALITY

To build the Yang force in your personality follow these steps:

1. Don't be a drifter in life. Have a definite course in which you are going toward your goals of achievement. Make up your mind that you will achieve success in your work and build a fortune. Magnetize your brain centers with suggestions that you can and will succeed. Make your demands on people and life, asking for that which is rightfully yours. Give your subconscious mind the following Yang auto-suggestions: I can succeed and have fame, fortune and fulfillment. I am a magnetic, charming person, showing a smiling, happy face and a radiant personality. I will overcome tendencies to weakness and inadequacy.

2. Build the magnetic quality of determination in your personality. This is a Yang force that helps you overcome the tendency to give in to life's challenges and obstacles. Have a blueprint of destiny on which you write down the things you want to achieve in your life. Each day, read this list over and be determined that you will be happy, that you will have romantic fulfillment, that you will become rich and successful. This magnetic force of determination will carry you through those difficult periods when things seem to go wrong and will build psychic energy to help you overcome life's defeats and disappointments.

Testimony No. 44

Linda D. Used Yang Qualities to Win a Husband at 45

Linda D. had been happily married for twenty-five years, and had two grown children, when her husband was killed in an accident. She found herself at forty-five years of age, still vitally energetic and desirous of a husband and companion. During all those years, she had been content to be just a housewife, and her husband had made all the decisions, taken care of the money and let Linda furnish him with a pleasant background in the home, caring for the children, fixing his meals and being a completely Yin type of personality: passive, submissive and without too much drive or ambition.

When she first told me that she wanted to marry again and have companionship and romance, she added quickly, "I know you probably think I'm too old for that sort of thing. My kids tell me to forget it, and my friends all think I'm crazy, but I'm lonely and I don't want to spend the rest of my life living alone."

I assured Linda that I believed she was right in having a desire to marry again. I then outlined a regimen which was a complete opposite to the life she had lived. I told her, "You must go out more. Join a church group or a social club, where there are parties and dances. Ignore the remarks of your children and your friends and make up your mind that you will find your romantic partner and marry again."

Without naming it, I was actually giving Linda a Yang routine of confidence and aggressiveness, which would help overcome the Yin tendency to withdraw and isolate herself.

The next time i saw Linda, she had made great progress. She even dressed differently, more youthfully with more make-up and a great deal more confidence. She told me she had joined a class in square dancing that a local social club had started. She had already met many friends and was no longer lonely and unhappy.

Within a period of two months, during which I saw Linda only once more, she was as happy and excited as a young bride. She told me that she had met a man who was a widower, a very successful businessman, who was dating her, and she knew that she was in love with him. In a few more weeks, I received a wedding invitation from Linda and when she walked down the aisle, there was an expression of joy on her face that showed me she had done the right thing! She changed her personality from Yin to Yang, and yet did not lose her feminine charms and appeal.

HOW TO BUILD A MAGNETIC PERSONALITY USING YANG QUALITIES

3. To help you overcome the negative Yin qualities of self-consciousness, inferiority and inadequacy, you must begin to build a new self image of poise, confidence and power in your personality. These are Yang qualities that will help you to achieve more magnetism and persuasiveness.

To help you build a more poised and powerful personality, stand before a mirror and observe yourself for fifteen minutes a day. Raise your head, as though wearing a crown. Keep your spine straight and your chin up. Breathe deeply so you will charge your brain with great quantities of positive magnetism, which is a Yang force. Then say to yourself or aloud the following Yang statements:

- I was born to have a great destiny.
- I am divine and unlimited, not human and limited.
- I now take on the crown of my divine kingdom and rule over the forces of life, causing them to obey my commands.
- I have a divine ego and am no longer fearful, inferior and inadequate in my dealings with others.
- I make my demands upon life and life repays me with success.
- I build qualities of peace, joy, beauty, good and love, and others respond on the same wavelength of magnetism.
- I am in the magic circle of God's divine love and protection. I am guided to my great destiny by divine intuition.

HOW I HELPED ELVIS PRESLEY WITH MY MAGNETIC MAGIC CIRCLE

Early in his career, the famous rock singer Elvis Presley came to look at my home in Bel-Air, with the idea of leasing it for a year. The first thing he said to me was, "I've heard that Howard Hughes lived in your home for a year, and also that Prince Rainier leased it while he was in Hollywood courting Grace Kelly. I sure would like to be able to live in a house where they lived."

It was true that Howard Hughes and Prince Rainier as well as many other world-famous celebrities did live in my home. Prince Rainier had called it "A miniature palace equal to my home in Monaco."

I could see that Elvis had a sincere desire to acquire culture and elegance. Although he was then making several million dollars a year, he realized that he must acquire acculturation of the mind before he could really take his place in the movie hall of fame as a truly great star.

As we walked through the house and finally came to the magnificent dining room, with its crystal chandeliers and the black and gold Regency furnishings, he stopped to admire two consoles at each end of the room, with antique mirrors over them. These swan-neck consoles were several hundred years old, hand carved from Italy and were in the rich black and gold regency style of the rest of the dining room.

Elvis paused for a moment, studying the swan-necked consoles and then he drawled, "I sure like them there ducks, I'll take the house."

I tell this true story, not to disparage Elvis, but to show admiration for that quality within him that made him want to acquire a cultural veneer that later would cause him to walk with presidents and kings.

In the months ahead, I came to know this sensitive young man quite well and I had the privilege of giving him my world famous Magic Circle, which I had given to more than five hundred famous Hollywood stars over the years.

Any feelings of inferiority that Elvis may have had due to his background and early training, certainly vanished when he acquired the Yang qualities of magnetism, confidence, poise, aggressiveness and charm. He then became the King of Hollywood!

A STUDY REGIME TO HELP YOU
BUILD YANG QUALITIES OF
MAGNETISM

To help you acquire a strong, poised and confident personality, it is necessary that you have a study regime which includes many different kinds of knowledge about many subjects. Acquire proficiency in speech, take a public speaking course to become more poised and fluent. Go to the library and study books on cultural subjects like art, music, literature and poetry. Become conversant with the latest books and their authors; know something about philosophy, psychology and current events as well as science and history. You will find that as you acquire more wisdom and knowledge, which are Yang forces, you will banish the Yin force of ignorance and become a balanced, dynamic and magnetic person capable of attracting a great destiny.

4.   One of the great Yang qualities which you will want to incorporate in your new self-image is that of courage to face life's challenges and to overcome fear of people and of life.

YANG MEDITATION TO HELP YOU
FACE LIFE'S CHALLENGES

To acquire courage, give yourself this meditation treatment each day before you begin your activities:

All day today I shall face life's challenges with courage and poise. I know that the law of passing time will remove all problems and obstacles and that I shall have the power to resist fear, worry and anxiety. I am now surrounded by the white light of God's infinite good and I can attract only good. I was born to a great destiny and I shall make of each experience in my life a stepping stone to greatness.

The Yin qualities of fear, anxiety, weak will, passivity and vacillation often obliterate the qualities of courage, strength, aggression and decisiveness, which are strong Yang qualities in a personality.

5.   To avoid the tendency to let other people make your decisions, you can develop the Yang qualities of leadership and power. Allowing others to choose your vocation, decide on your gifts and talents, select your level of income and dictate how you shall live your life is to be constantly in a state of indecision and confusion.

HOW YOU CAN ACQUIRE THE
YANG QUALITIES OF LEADERSHIP
AND SUPERIORITY

You can go into the inner realm and discover the unlimited horizons of the mind. Use the following meditation to give you the Yang qualities of leadership, dominance, inspiration and superiority.

I now shape my thinking in the direction of leadership and power. I set high standards for achievement in the future. I consult my own psychic mind centers for the right course of action in my life. I avoid thinking mass thoughts of commonness, low standards, obscenity, vulgarity and selfishness. I rise into the spiritual stratosphere of beauty, idealism and good, and my actions follow suit. I become a leader, not a follower, and I aim my sights towards the noble and magnificent experiences of life.

Testimony No. 45

How a Young Plumber Used the Power of Yang to Choose a New Career

An example of how others can often shape our destinies was that of Harold C. who came into our studies in New York City. His father was a plumber who was making very good money, so when Harold graduated high school his father urged him to come into the business with him. Harold tried to be interested in the business but his mind was on other things. He loved the outdoors, he wanted to go into something connected with horticulture and farming. He spent his weekends on camping trips where he could be outdoors. He felt stifled in his work and began to work through the mystical laws he had learned in our classes to gain liberation from the work he hated. He projected a new life for himself, doing work he liked.

One day his father sent him on a repair job to a place out on Long Island. It was one of the biggest greenhouses in that area, specializing in growing miniature trees, house plants, flowers and shrubs. Harold was fascinated by the various aspects of this business. In talking to the owner, he found there was an opening in the business for another partner. As he had saved several thousand dollars, Harold decided he would buy a share in the business. His father told him he was crazy, but the young man went ahead and made his investment. He soon found that it was a thriving business and in a few months time, returned his entire investment. But more important than the money was the fact that Harold had at last found work he was interested in. In three years, Harold had made so much money that he was able to buy a beautiful home on Long Island. He married a young lady he had met through his work a year before, they settled into his new home and are now on the way to rearing a fine family. His dreams were fulfilled because he followed his own intuition as to what his destiny was to be.

HOW TO BUILD THE YANG QUALITY OF OPTIMISM IN YOUR PERSONALITY

6.   Pessimism is a Yin quality and optimism is a Yang quality. If you habitually look on the dark side of life and are filled with fear, worry and anxiety, these negative Yin forces will neutralize your ambitions, paralyze your will power and short circuit your magnetism. To treat this tendency to look on the dark side of life, use the following Yang meditation:

> *Every day, I affirm that I am strong and able to meet my duties and obligations in life with hope and optimism. I see the bright side of every situation. I have faith in myself and my great destiny. I aim at the stars of life and I achieve my high goals. I am cheerful and optimistic, even when things go wrong. I know that I shall be guided by my higher, intuitive mind to the fulfillment of my dreams.*

7.   When you act from impulsiveness to every situation in life rather than with rationality and reason, you are apt to have constant problems in your life. Confucius taught that there must be order in the mind first, and then there will be order in your environment. When you are mentally calm and orderly you can think things through in a rational manner and avoid many of life's mistakes.

HOW TO USE THE ORIENTAL SYSTEM OF YIN-YANG FOR PEACE OF MIND

Thousands of people are emotionally breaking down today and require psychiatric treatment because they let their emotions get out of control. The Oriental system of control causes one to sit in stillness and visualize the mind like a lake. When thoughts are turbulent and confused, the surface of the lake has huge waves on it. Sit in meditation and think or say the following to overcome such emotional turbulence and disorientation:

> *The surface of my mind is now like a still lake, reflecting the beauty of the golden sun and the blue skies. Not a ripple on the surface of my mental lake. All my thoughts are now under perfect control. My emotions are now controlled. I think thoughts of peace and my life becomes peaceful. I think thoughts of joy and my life reflects situations that bring enjoyment.*

I think and act in a friendly manner and I make friends who are on the same wavelength as I am.
I am now in the magic circle aura of power and poise and my inner and outer life become peaceful, poised and powerful. I am in the driver's seat of thought and my ship of state arrives safely in the harbor of self-realization and fulfillment.

8. Today, millions of people accept the situations into which they were born with passivity and fatalism. They believe that they cannot change things; they depend on the politicians in Washington to do their thinking for them. As children, we were dependent on our parents for guidance. As we mature, we are supposed to do our own thinking and act out the pattern of destiny we consciously select. No person need be limited by circumstances of birth, lack of education or economic conditions. Even during the depression of the thirties, some people became millionaires. Since World War II there have been more than 25,000 new millionaires in this country.

YANG MEDITATION TO HELP YOU ACQUIRE RICHES AND FULFILLMENT OF DESTINY

To overcome the inertia of failure, limitation and poverty, give yourself the following meditation for riches and fulfillment of destiny:

I now affirm that I am a thinking, creative being, capable of creating the destiny I desire. I wish to rise above the limited plane of consciousness that keeps me tied to failure, frustration and poverty. I now invoke the mental law of alchemy that can turn my thoughts into the shimmering gold of reality. I ask my higher mind to guide me to the finding of my true destiny. I desire an overall goal of half a million dollars or more to furnish my family and myself with financial security for the rest of our lives. I ask for the release of gifts and talents that will cause me to rise above the limitations of my present environment. I wish to become famous, powerful and rich. I shall use my money intelligently to improve the world and benefit humanity.

THE YIN-YANG FOODS FOR HEALTH AND LONG LIFE

There are certain foods that are acid and others that are alkaline in their effect on the body. The Ancients called these two types of food Yin and Yang. They advocated a diet in which there were 75 percent of alkaline or Yang foods, and only 25 percent of acid or Yin foods.

Following are the Yin and Yang foods that are the most important in a diet. Most vegetables and fruits fall into the Yang classification. Most meats and dairy products fall into the Yin classification. After checking this list you can easily determine into which category other foods fall:

YIN FOODS

CAKES AND PIES
SUGAR (white sugar)
WHITE RICE (Brown rice is
   more Yang than Yin)
WHITE BREAD AND
   WHITE FLOUR
ICE CREAM AND MOST
   SUGAR MADE DESSERTS
RED BLOODED MEATS,
   BEEF, PORK, STEAKS
MILK AND MILK
   PRODUCTS, CHEESE
EGGS
SALT, SPICES, CATSUP,
   VINEGAR
COFFEE, TEA, ALCOHOL

YANG FOODS

WHOLE GRAINS
BROWN RICE
BROWN SUGAR,
   HONEY
BREADS MADE WITH
   WHOLE WHEAT OR
   OTHER FRESH WHOLE GRAINS
FISH AND FOWL ARE PART
   YIN AND PART YANG
NATURAL HERBS, HERB
   TEAS
FRUITS AND VEGETABLES
   OF ALL KINDS

Many Orientals are vegetarians as meat is scarce, but those who follow this Yin-Yang diet eat *only* 25 percent of meats and other Yin foods and the other 75 percent of the diet consists of Yang foods, which are vegetables, fruits and whole grains.

Eggs are often eaten as a source of protein and milk is used widely, but these are both Yin foods and should be taken in moderation. Now, with our modern knowledge of cholesterol, we know that meat, eggs and milk in large quantities contain too much of this substance and should be restricted in a diet.

As citrus fruits and juices are Yang foods, they can be taken in small daily amounts with great benefits to a balanced diet.

Honey, fruits, dates and figs can be substituted for ice cream, cakes and pies.

Vegetable juices of all kinds are Yang in nature and can be taken in moderate amounts daily.

It is obvious that all Yin foods cannot be cut out, for the diet would then be unbalanced. Therefore, good judgment must be used to maintain the 25 percent balance of Yin foods with the 75 percent of Yang foods. In this way, you can even become a vegetarian and substitute eggs, nuts and protein vegetables (brown rice has much protein) for meats and still obtain sufficient protein to keep the body in good health.

MYSTO-MATIC POINTERS

1. *Each day, make it a point to emphasize the positive qualities that make you magnetic and persuasive. These qualities are optimism, cheerfulness, hope, faith, good, joy and love.*

2. *Maintain a mental balance by refusing to react too emotionally to life's stresses and strains.*

3. *Build vast storehouses of wisdom and knowledge by studying throughout your life. Knowledge is Yang and gives you great magnetism.*

4. *Overcome the debilitating forces of fear, worry, hate, revenge, jealousy and greed. These are Yin forces that short circuit your brain and body magnetism.*

5. *Express the Yang emotion of love daily in your contacts with others, and show tolerance for their weaknesses and understanding of their shortcomings.*

6. *Have a positive mental attitude towards life and people. Try to see the best side of every situation not the bad side.*

7. *Use positive words in your contacts with others and refrain from being critical, sarcastic and negative in your remarks.*

8. *Act with confidence and poise in every situation; the world admires a confident person who knows what he wants in life.*

9. *Have high ideals and standards and avoid being vulgar, obscene and common in your speech and actions.*

10. *Have a balance of the masculine and feminine qualities in your personality rather than being overly masculine or overly feminine.*

12

THE SACRED EGYPTIAN FLAME RITUAL FROM THE TEMPLE OF OSIRIS BURNS YOUR DREAMS INTO REALITY

From Egypt, the ancient land of mystery and magic, there has been revealed one of the great secrets of all time, which you can use to make your dreams come true.

This is the secret of the Egyptian Flame Ritual that was discovered in the Temple of Osiris by recent explorers. On one of my visits to Egypt several years ago I obtained a literal translation of this Flame Ritual, which was found in the Temple of Osiris. A group of my students who were with me began to use this

RITUAL TO THE FLAME with astounding success. Miracles of healing occurred. Some developed latent gifts and talents which they had requested from the sacred flame. Still others asked for large sums of money and their requests were granted in the most amazing ways. One woman had not been able to conceive a child for several years and she wrote her request on a piece of paper, consigned it to the sacred flame, and within one year she bore a healthy, normal child!

A SCIENTIST CAUSED WARTS TO DISAPPEAR BY USING THE FLAME RITUAL

A scientist recently tested this magical power of the flame with twenty children who had warts all over their hands. He had them draw pictures of their palms on paper, placing the warts in position on their hands. He then told the children he was burning the paper in an urn and that their warts would all disappear within a few days. He mumbled some invocation over the flame as the paper burned while the children concentrated on the ritual. Within a period of two weeks all the warts on the children's hands had disappeared!

What was the magic power released by the invocation to the flame? Scientists do not know, but they do know that there are mysterious forces in the universe which seem to work like magic when these higher powers are invoked.

The discoveries of the golden treasures of King Tutankhamon that are on tour throughout the world, have revealed strange and unusual powers that can be summoned up which have been called white magic and black magic. The ancient Egyptians believed that a curse could release black magic that would work harm to those who violated spiritual laws. They also believed that white magic could release blessings for those who worked in cooperation with the spiritual forces in the universe.

YOUR MIND CAN RELEASE A CURSE OR A BLESSING

Your higher psychic mind has the power to release a curse or a blessing in your life. If you obey the spiritual laws of the universe, you will work with them and white magic or blessings will occur in your life.

You are now going to learn how to use the Egyptian Flame Ritual from the Temple of Osiris to work miracles of white magic in your life. You can also use this dynamic mystical power to protect you from danger and to insulate you against the recurring misfortunes of the outer world.

REGIMEN FOR USING THE SACRED
EGYPTIAN FLAME RITUAL
TO MAKE YOUR DREAMS COME
TRUE

1.　To invoke the mystical power of the Egyptian Flame Ritual, you must prepare a shrine where you can do the invocation to the sacred flame and not be disturbed while doing it. This can be in any quiet corner of your house or apartment. Have a white candle burning, a sacred symbol of a cross, or the Key of Life, which is a cross with a circle over it. You can also have a miniature pyramid on your shrine to focus the dynamic power in your environment.

2.　Have a small metal tray on which you can burn your pieces of paper, with your requests written on them. If you wish, you can also have incense burning to give a fragrance to the room. You will note in most modern churches this Sacred Flame Ritual is performed automatically, with incense burning, candles lighted at the altar and the invocations given by priests or modern ministers for blessings to be showered upon members of the congregation.

WRITE DOWN YOUR REQUESTS
FOR THE SACRED FLAME

3.　After you have set up your sacred shrine, you can write down your requests on a piece of paper, which you are going to burn with the invocation to the Sacred flame. These requests can be as follows, or you can make up your own. Ask as many things as you desire; some of them may be granted quickly, others may take longer, depending on the nature of the request. Sample requests:

- I desire the sum of $10,000 to meet my needs.
- I wish to have a complete healing of my body.
- I ask for my true soul mate for love and marriage.
- Grant me the fulfillment of my desire for a dream home.

- I wish to own a new car.
- Give me the gift of creative art for—(here state if you wish it to become an author, artist, composer, inventor or anything else you desire.)
- Help me solve my present problems, so I can be free of worry.
- Heal my friend (or relative) of the illness she suffers from.
- Help me find peace of mind and freedom from anxiety.

- I wish to take a vacation trip to Europe; how can I obtain the money for this trip?

4.   You can write down any number of requests on the sheet of paper. When you have done so, sign your name.

5.   Now you can prepare the urn to receive your list of requests, as you now ignite the piece of paper at the burning white candle, you will recite the following invocation to the Flame as the paper burns.

> *I now invoke the power of the sacred flame to grant me the following requests which I have inscribed on this piece of paper.*
> *I believe in the miracle of the flame. I now invoke the miracle-working power of the Sun God Osiris. I recognize that the sun is the power behind life, giving us energy and creating the miracle of growth in the soil. I also recognize that behind the physical sun there is a spiritual sun called God, whom I now invoke, asking that He bless my life with the requests that I have made.*

5.   Then, as the piece of paper burns and turns into ashes you can once again intone:

I believe in the miracle of the flame and it is done unto me according to my faith.

6.   Your initiation into the mysteries of the Egyptian Flame ritual can give you a tremendous sense of power and achievement. You will begin to see some of the things you requested come true right away and this will give you greater faith in the miracle-working power of the Sacred Flame. However, do not stop after having performed the ritual once. You should renew this exercise at least once a week, putting the same requests into the flame or adding new ones.

Testimony No. 46

How Tyrone G. Projected a Yacht in the Flame Ritual

Tyrone G. was a new student in our classes in California, and he used the Egyptian Flame ritual to ask for the one thing he had dreamed of for years: To own his own boat. He lived in a place called Newport Beach, where John Wayne had his home, and it was Tyrone's desire to have a boat which he could use for entertaining his friends and also for fishing and water sports.

It took two months for Tyrone's request to be granted; he then found out that the city of Newport was putting up some boats that had been discarded for auction. Only two people bid on the boats and Tyrone obtained his beautiful motor boat that would sleep six people for an amazingly low sum!

Then, Tyrone began to give other requests to the flame, one being that he would receive a better job with more money, so he could afford the luxury of a boat. He soon obtained a job as manager of a boat building and repair shop where he could use his knowledge of boats to good advantage and his salary made it possible to maintain his boat in style.

The next request Tyrone made was that he find his true soul mate, so he could have someone to share his beautiful new life. A few days later, the daughter of a very wealthy man came into the place where Tyrone worked, seeking a new boat for her father. She and Tyrone struck up a friendship that led to a beautiful romance, and six months later, they had a magnificent wedding on her father's new yacht. Tyrone's life changed miraculously after he began to use the Sacred Flame Ritual from the Temple of Osiris.

USE THE FLAME RITUAL TO TURN
BLACK MAGIC FORCES INTO
WHITE MAGIC FORCES

7.   If there seem to be bad luck cycles in your life, which you suspect may be projections of black magic from enemies, you can use the sacred flame ritual to turn this black magic into white magic. When you do your flame ritual, write these words down on a piece of paper: I now invoke the Sacred Flame to remove this curse that seems to be in my life. I now return the evil projections back to the source and I am free of all effects of black magic. I now attract only good luck and white magic forces. Then, burn the piece of paper in the sacred flame and be confident that you will no longer be under a black magic spell of bad luck and curses.

Testimony No. 47

How Adele F. Broke an Evil Spell With the Flame Ritual

Adele F. was married to a man for ten years and they had always gotten along very well. One night, at a party, Adele's husband was introduced by the hostess to a very flashily dressed blonde who seemed to immediately show an interest in him

Within two week's time Adele had proof that her husband was seeing this woman. She confronted him with the evidence and he admitted it and told her that he was no longer happy in his marriage and wanted a divorce.

Adele consulted me about this problem and I told her about the Egyptian Flame ritual and its power for breaking a spell of black magic. This other woman was obviously using her sexual attractions to cast a spell on Adele's husband.

Adele was told to write down on a piece of paper the following invocation to the flame:

I now ask that the spell being cast by _____ (Here she put down the other woman's name) over my husband be broken, so he will give her up and return to me. I do not wish revenge, but I ask for my marriage to continue happily as it did in the past.

After Adele burned this paper in the flame she had complete confidence that her husband would return to her. He had already moved in with the other woman and had consulted a lawyer about getting a divorce from his wife.

One night, two weeks after she had done the flame ritual, her telephone rang. When Adele answered it she found it was her husband. He told her that he wanted to see her right away. Although it was two in the morning, Adele agreed to see him. Her husband's right hand was bandaged and when Adele asked him what had happened he told her a strange tale. It seemed that the blonde woman had been visited by one of her old boy friends and when he left, Adele's husband accused the woman of infidelity. In a fit of rage the woman had taken a butcher knife and slashed at him, cutting his hand severely. He had gone to the hospital to have it sewn up and then had refused to press charges, but he did not return to the other woman's apartment again.

Adele forgave her husband and they reunited. She saw the miracle of the flame work its magic power, for she and her husband remained together, and their love was stronger than ever.

HOW TO USE WHITE MAGIC TO
INFLUENCE OTHERS FOR GOOD

8. You can also use the white magic represented by the sacred flame to influence the minds of others and cause them to do your wishes. This power should be used only for good, however, for if it is used for evil purposes it becomes black magic and will destroy the person misusing it

BLACK MAGIC FORCES
DESTROYED HUNDREDS AT
GUYANA

An example of how black magic can be used for purposes of evil was that of the tragedy of Guyana, where Jim Jones literally cast a spell over the minds of his followers, causing them to go to their deaths with him in the jungles of South America. It is never good to let anyone control your mind for their own evil purposes. This type of mass hypnotism and black magic was used by Hitler and it caused the deaths of millions. Black magic was also used by Charles Manson, when he controlled the members of his "family" and made them kill for the cause.

If you have a legitimate purpose for using white magic, you can invoke this power for good. Let us see how it was used for good by a member of our lecture work.

Testimony No. 48

Raymond R. Used the Flame Ritual
to Get Back Money He Loaned

Raymond R. was owed the sum of $2,000 by a man who had borrowed it, promising to return it with interest in six months. The man let two years go by and never returned Raymond's money. It was then that I told Raymond to use the Sacred Flame Ritual with this invocation:

> *I now ask of the Sacred Flame that this man _____ (Here he gave his name) be influenced to return the sum of $2,000 that he borrowed from me. I ask only for his good fortune and good luck.*

Within three weeks, this man entered Raymond's office and dumped a large sum of money on his desk. It turned out to be $4,000, or double what Raymond had loaned him. The man then explained that he had gone into a small business with the loan, and was now beginning to make big money. He offered to give Raymond a percentage of his profits every month for the next year!

HOW TO USE THE FLAME RITUAL
FOR HEALING SICKNESS

9.   You can also use the Sacred Flame Ritual for purposes of healing yourself or others. Write down on a piece of paper the specific condition you believe you are suffering from, as follows:

I am suffering from an inflamed gall bladder. I now ask the Sacred Flame to give me a complete healing of this condition so I shall not need an operation.

Testimony No. 49

Edith F. Used the Flame Ritual to Avoid Surgery

Edith F. had an inflamed gall bladder when she asked me if she could use the Flame Ritual to bring about a healing. I told her that many people had reported miracle healings through this ritual. She prepared the piece of paper and wrote on it as above, and then consigned it to the sacred flame as she did the invocation.

Within a month's time the symptoms of gall bladder inflammation had stopped altogether. When Edith returned to her doctor and he took tests, he reported that she did not need an operation, for in some mysterious manner, the condition had healed itself!

USE THE FLAME RITUAL TO
OVERCOME HABITS OF SMOKING
OR ALCOHOLISM

10.   You can also use the invocation to the Sacred Flame for purposes of breaking bad habits such as smoking, drinking, overeating, drug addiction or other negative habits that are harmful to your health or life.

Write down on a piece of paper something like the following invocation:

I now ask the Sacred Flame to rid me of the following negative habit. I smoke excessively and I know it is harmful to my health. I wish to have this habit broken.

If it is some other habit, then name it on the piece of paper, and consign it to the sacred flame with this invocation.

I have faith in the power of the Sacred Flame. I now gain strength and courage so I can master this negative habit. I feel a sense of freedom and relief that this habit is now broken.

Testimony No. 50

Burton T. Overcame Drug Dependence With the Flame Ritual

Burton T. had gotten into the habit of taking sleeping pills when he could not sleep at night and was soon addicted to them. Then, to give him pep and energy during the day he took other forms of medication. Soon he had formed a dependence on these drugs and he became moody and depressed. He often thought of committing suicide. It was in this desperate state that a friend of his brought him to our lecture work and he learned about the Sacred Flame ritual.

Burton T. wrote the habit that was slowly destroying him down on a piece of paper. He was told to do the ritual every day for the next month, or until he had gained enough strength to kick his habit. Before the month was over, Burton was sleeping without the aid of medication, and in a short time, he did not need the pep pills that were causing him to go into slumps of moodiness and suicidal depression. He was cured of his habit entirely and became mentally and physically healthy.

MYSTO-MATIC POINTERS

1. *Do not use this Egyptian Flame Ritual to get revenge on other people or to wish them harm. Black magic forces come back to harm one, so only use this ritual for good.*

2. *If some person is doing you harm, you can write the name of the person on a piece of paper with this request: I ask that this person be removed to his or her right place where only good can come to them.*

3. *If you wish to have a specific sum of money for a purpose write down the sum like: I desire the sum of $5,000 to*

*help me meet my payments. Then burn this in the flame
with the mystic chant already given.*

4. *If you wish to use the flame ritual for healing, write down
   the condition on a piece of paper and burn it in the flame,
   saying: I now ask that this illness be healed completely.*

5. *Use the flame ritual at least once a week. It can do no
   harm.*

6. *When some requests have been granted write down
   others and use the flame ritual to bring these to
   fulfillment.*

7. *You can ask protection and guidance from the Flame
   ritual by writing down this request: I now ask for divine
   protection for my family and myself in all our affairs of
   life.*

13

LIFE'S TEN GREATEST
TREASURES THROUGH
FANTASTIC MYSTIC POWER

Life's ten greatest treasures can easily be yours if you use your mystic powers to attract them into your daily life. These treasures are worth more than mere money, for they relate to the permanent riches of the universe. You may tap these treasures by following a regimen of mystical contemplation and rituals that can focus transcendental power in your higher psychic mind centers.

We shall now learn how to release mystical powers to bring you peace of mind, vibrant good health, happiness, riches and abundance on every plane of existence.

TREASURE NO. 1—DIVINE
GUIDANCE THROUGH INNER
PERCEPTION

God has given you one of the greatest of all gifts: The treasure of your own higher psychic mind centers through which you can be guided by the voice of divine intuition.

You can ask this Higher Psychic mind to guide you to your right work. You can petition it to shower you with gifts of money, power, fame, love happiness, your right work, friends and social life, good health and long life. This Divine Power within your own psychic mind centers wants you to have all these things and more in life.

To consult this higher divine mind within you, sit in the stillness and recite the mystical mantra from Tibet, *Aum mane padme aum.* As you now know, this means the jewel in the heart of the Lotus and refers to the soul-center within yourself and the soul of the universe.

By reciting this mystical mantra ten times slowly and in rhythm, you will attune your higher psychic mind centers to the over-soul of the universe which knows all, sees all and is all.

HOW TO SWITCH ON THE MYSTO-
PSYCHIC SCREEN WITHIN YOUR
MIND

There is, within your own psychic mind, what the mystics call The Third Eye. This is located approximately in the center of your forehead and is to be visualized as a third eye within your own brain. When you sit in meditation to receive the benefits of inner psychic perception and divine guidance, you will visualize a screen stretching across your forehead, within your own brain; you will learn now to focus psycho-astral rays on this mental psychic screen, just as you see television pictures focused on your set.

Now visualize an astral ray of brilliant white light coming from the celestial heights. Focus this beam of light on your psychic screen and with it draw or write down the things that you want your higher psychic mind to bring you. For example: You desire a dream home, so let that white light now draw out the picture of your perfect dream home in every detail. Write down the words I DESIRE first, and then spell out the words MY DREAM HOME. You can do this letter by letter just as a flashing neon sign in modern advertising spells out a word or makes a picture.

If you have a picture of your dream home which you have cut out of some magazine, you can focus your mind on this a few moments before you go into psychic meditation to create the dream home on your Mysto-psychic screen.

Now flash that dream home onto your psychic screen, room by room, complete with all the furnishings. See its location in the country, see the garden, the fenced-in yard for the children, then walk through the rooms seeing them in every detail.

This psychic exercise is more than just day dreaming; it is the method by which you program your higher mind centers with the actual material objects you wish to attract.

Now give yourself the following Mysto-Psychic meditation to project that dream home to the outer world of reality:

> *I now project the psychic picture of my perfect dream home. I desire this home for my family and myself. I ask my higher psychic mind centers to reveal to me the method by which I can obtain this perfect dream home.*

Testimony No. 51

A Dream Home Appears Out of the Blue

Dolores and John M. had a deep desire for a dream home. They projected this dream home on their Mysto-Psychic screen for several days, using the above meditation statement.

One Sunday as they were driving through Long Island, something caused them to stop before a house that seemed to be their Dream Home. As they sat in their car looking, an elderly lady came out and said to them, "I noticed you sitting here for some time and I wondered if I could help you?"

They then told her they were admiring her home and wanted to buy one just like it. The woman then said, "It's strange you should say that, for I have been planning to put my home up for sale."

They talked it over for a while and found she would sell it to them for a very small down payment, including all the furnishings! They made the deal and within a month, Dolores and John moved into their perfect dream home!

HOW TO PROJECT VARIOUS SUMS OF MONEY ONTO YOUR PSYCHIC SCREEN

If you wish to project sums of money on this psychic screen, write out the various sums, preceding them with the words, I DESIRE. Then, see the sum flashing like a neon sign—on and off—$5,000 or $10,000 or $50,000. After you have visualized the psycho-astral ray writing out the sum of money you need, say the following mystic invocation to your higher psychic mind:

I desire the sum of $50,000 to meet my immediate and future needs. I ask for psychic guidance as to how I shall obtain this sum of money.

When you come out of your psychic session, go about your ordinary everyday activities. You may not immediately see results, for the higher psychic mind must make contact with the cosmic mind that rules the universe before you can be personally guided to the method for obtaining that sum of money.

Testimony No. 52

Susan E. Won the $50,000 Lottery Through Psychic Power

Susan E., one of my students in New York City, desperately wanted money for a certain project. Her father had recently died, leaving debts after his funeral expenses and she and her mother could hardly get along on Susan's small salary. In psychic meditation she daily wrote out the sum of $50,000 on her psychic screen. One day she passed a stand that sold lottery tickets. She had never bought a ticket in her life but something impelled her to stop and buy half a dozen tickets. She pocketed them, praying that one of them would be a winner.

When the results of the lottery drawing were announced Susan found that she had one of the winning tickets for exactly the sum she had asked for, $50,000!

It is no mere coincidence that in our New York lecture group, in one year, three different members who bought lottery tickets drew sums varying from $10,000 to $100,000! They had all used this method of Mysto-Psychic screen projection!

One man who won the million dollar ticket in New Jersey announced to the press that he had projected a psychic image through a dream he had of the winning number in the lottery! He was instinctively using this Mysto-Psychic Screen method to project his Desires for riches and abundance to the Cosmic Mind that rules the universe.

HOW TO PROJECT YOUR IDEAL
SOUL MATE THROUGH PSYCHIC
POWER

If you are trying to project your ideal soul mate through the Mysto-Psychic Screen method, you can mentally flash onto that screen a composite picture of the mate you would consider ideal. See the face, expressing the personality you consider perfect; see the coloration of eyes and hair, the qualities the person possesses. Or, if it is someone you know that you wish to magnetize and cause to fall in love with you, project that person's face onto your psychic screen and write out the name in flashing letters on the screen, with this meditation statement:

> *I desire the ideal soul mate with these qualities of kindness, gentility, culture, loyalty and spirituality. I ask that I be guided to my perfect soul mate and that I shall recognize the person when we meet.*

Testimony No. 53

How Clarice J. Projected Her Ideal Soul Mate
on the Mysto-Psychic Screen

One of my lecture members in Los Angeles, Clarice J. had long desired her true soul mate. She was twenty-four and felt that she could not afford to waste any more time in waiting. She projected the ideal man as having auburn hair and blue eyes; she saw him as tall and athletically built, well educated and attractive.

Clarice sat in meditation and projected this psychic dream for only one week. Then, one day as she was driving down Hollywood Boulevard, a car struck her from the rear and ruined the back of her car. She sustained a whiplash and was taken to the hospital where X-rays were taken showing minor injuries. She was forced to wear a neck brace for some time. She sought out a lawyer to help her institute a lawsuit against the driver of the other car. When she walked into the lawyer's office, she saw a handsome young man, about thirty years of age, with auburn hair, blue eyes and a bright smiling face that was the ideal soul mate she had psychically projected!

The young man was single, made a date with her, fell in love with her and they had a beautiful wedding, to which I was invited! Her psychic soul mate was waiting for her, and she was guided to finding him through her psychic programming.

TREASURE NO. 2—SELF-RECOGNITION: REVELATIONS OF THE "I AM" CONSCIOUSNESS

Another great gift that God has given you is the "I Am" consciousness, which makes you realize that you have a spark of Divinity within your own immortal soul. You have been given the gift of self-awareness on the highest planes of consciousness.

To channel this Awesome power of the mighty "I Am," sit in meditation, and recite the mystic mantra *Aum mane padme aum,* repeating it ten times. Then close your eyes and say a meditation like the following; or you can read this one until you are able to originate your own:

I now enter the mystical threshold of the mighty "I Am" consciousness and take on the powers of the creative cosmic mind. I am imbued with the creative spirit of good and my life reflects only good. "I Am" created in the image and likeness of God therefore I cannot be inferior, inadequate, self-conscious or limited in any way. I become superior and invincible. "I Am" imbued with the creative principle of divine love and I become loving, forgiving, charitable and creative. "I Am" protected in times of danger and I rise above the problems of life into the stratosphere of pure spiritual essence where "I Am" perpetually in the light of peace, beauty, harmony, joy and good. "I Am" that which "I Am," and no negative force can deny me my great spiritual destiny.

HOW THE "I AM" PRESENCE CAN
FORM A PSYCHO-RADAR SCREEN
TO PROTECT YOU FROM ALL
DANGER

When you have fears of bodily harm or danger, you can use the "I Am" presence to protect you, just as though you had a psycho-radar shield around your body, which deflects harm.

As you sit in meditation, to emphasize the "I Am" principle, visualize a circle of white light around your body, which is your spiritual aura. Place this white light shield around yourself as you walk through dark streets or face any situations in which danger might exist and then affirm:

> *I am surrounded by the white light of God's infinite presence. A thousand shall fall on my right and ten thousand on my left, but shall not come near me. Only with mine eyes shall I behold the rewards of the wicked.*

Eyes, in the sense, refers to the inner spiritual consciousness, that recognizes the punishment that goes to the wicked and the rewards that go to the righteous, who live under God's cosmic laws.

PSYCHIC SOMNAMBULISM TO
LESSEN LIFE'S PAINS AND
TRAGEDIES

You can also practice an exercise from the Far East known as Psychic Somnambulism, or the Dreamless Sleep of Sushupti, in which you go into a trance-like state, like a sleep walker, whenever you face any difficult or dangerous situation in life. By putting yourself in this state of Psychic Somnambulism you will be able to lessen the pain of difficult or tragic situations in life, such as the death of a loved one, a painful operation, or a sudden shock, such as a divorce or the loss of your children through legal action. Put yourself into a meditation state by reciting the mystical mantra *Aum mane padme aum*, and then think or say the following meditation statement:

> *I now enter into the state of psychic somnambulism in which I withdraw my mind and perceptions from the outer world of pain, suffering and tragedy. I withdraw into the innermost cathedral of the soul where I am safe and immune from the winds of misfortune that blow in the outer world. I affirm my spiritual reality of the*

*dream behind life, and I now live in the dream and reality
withdraws from my sense perceptions, bringing me security, peace
and safety.*

TREASURE NO. 3—THE JOY OF
LOVE AND PARENTHOOD

One of life's greatest treasures is to know true love and to be able to use
that love creatively and procreatively to produce a child in your own image and
likeness. This priceless gift has been given to all human beings and it makes
them fulfill the promise made in the bible, "Let us make man in our image and
likeness; and in His image and likeness created He them." You have been given
the divine emotion of love so you may share in the creative spirit that manifests
in the universe, bringing forth billions of forms of life so that man may better
enjoy God's miraculous universe.

MYSTIC MEDITATION TO FIND
LOVE FULFILLMENT

To focus this divine emotion in your higher consciousness, and cause it to
bring you life's rich rewards, go into quiet meditation and say the sacred mantra
ten times, then think or read the following statement:

*I now contemplate the divine mystery into which I was born. Out of
the mists of time and space my soul was born in the divine image
and likeness of God through the emotion of love. I now manifest
that divine love in every facet of my being and create in my own image and likeness, giving life, power and beauty to my own creations.
I give thanks for this priceless treasure, for God is Love.*

You can use the above meditation if you have romantic problems or if you
have not yet attracted your true soul mate and wish to do so. Go into meditation
every day for a few moments and concentrate on the image of ideal love,
repeating the above statement several times.

TREASURE NO. 4—VIBRANT
GOOD HEALTH AND A LONG LIFE

Good health with energy and vitality to meet your every daily need is one
of God's greatest blessings. When you have health you can soon have wealth,

happiness and all the good things of life. If you are sick and in pain and your life expectancy is short, then you have indeed been robbed of one of the greatest treasures on earth.

There are many facets to good health, including the right diet, plenty of mild exercise, rest and relaxation, avoidance of stress situations in your daily life, happiness in love and marriage, a balanced life between work and play, love and worship of God.

MEDITATION FOR ACHIEVING
VITAL GOOD HEALTH

You can use the following meditation to attune your mind and body to the higher wavelengths of cosmic energy that can bring you good health and assure you of living as long as you wish to live:

I now meditate on establishing the connection between cosmic mind and my mind, which can bring me energy and vitality, with good health and a long, useful life. I breathe deeply of the pranic life force and it now courses through my body, bringing me energy, youth, vitality and healing of all negative conditions. I now relax my mind and body, removing all stress from my nerve centers. I am now attuned to the cosmic mind that created me and which knows how to sustain me in perfect health throughout my entire life.

TREASURE NO. 5—WORK THAT
YOU ENJOY AND WHICH
REWARDS YOU

As most of your life will be spent in doing some kind of work, it is vitally important that you select work you can enjoy and which will reward you in some way besides money.

To be able to release your great potentials for finding your right work or going into your own business, you can go into meditation, enlisting the aid of your higher psychic mind and intuition. Use the following meditation for this:

I now release the power potentials of my higher creative mind and ask that I be guided to my right life work. I wish to be in work that gives me joy and which helps the world. I ask for rewards from my work and ask that I am guided to finding the talents that will be

*used for the good of others as well as to bring me financial rewards
and future security for my family and myself.*

Testimony No. 54

Viola K. Invoked Mystic Power to Build a New Career in Art

An example of how Mystic power can release new creative talents is that of a woman named Viola K. who had recently become a widow with two small children to look after. She had never learned any trade, having married early and being content to remain a housewife. She was now faced with the necessity of taking care of her children. She lived near an art school and, before her husband had died, she took evening art lessons when the children were taken care of by her husband. She had no special talents, but she relaxed and enjoyed the social contacts she made with beginning young artists and teachers.

One day, in reading the personals in the newspaper, she saw a small ad asking for workers who could do photo coloring at home. She applied, obtained the complete kit and some sample photos and had soon excelled so greatly in this art that she was able to finish as many as ten to fifteen big photographs a week. They looked like original oil paintings of the persons and the photo studio charged $50 for each one framed, and gave Loretta $10 for each photo. As this was prior to the days of inflation, it represented a very large income, and she was able to pay all her expenses and work at home, where she could still attend to the needs of her two children. In a short time, Loretta had added other photographic studios to her list and was doubling her output, bringing in a bigger income than her husband had when he was alive!

THE PSYCHIC MONEY PRESS
EXERCISE TO BRING YOUR RICHES

There is a wonderful mystic exercise that you can use to bring you all the money you will ever need in the future. As riches flow from the creative ideas you have within your own mind, you will utilize this principle in your psychic money press exercise.

To begin the psychic money press, first cut out ten pieces of white paper, the size and shape of a dollar bill. Now in the four corners of these pieces of paper put the numbers of the sums of money you wish to demonstrate. You can start with a thousand dollar bill, so write $1,000 in the four corners of the paper.

Now you can mentally print ten of these pieces of paper marked with the $1,000 in the four corners. Now count them out and you will have the sum of $10,000.

Mentally, you will now visualize a printing press with blank paper flowing through it. Close your eyes and project the images on that money press as $1,000 bills. See the press printing hundreds of these bills. Then visualize yourself taking as many of these bills as you need for some specific project. See yourself paying money down for a new home; visualize yourself paying for a new car, or buying a color TV set, or furnishings for the home. As you do this mental exercise with your psychic money press, give yourself this meditation statement:

> *I now project on my psychic money press a perpetual flow of money to give me security for the future. I project $100,000 to give me all the things I desire. I project $500,000 for a lifetime of riches and abundance and enjoyment. I project smaller sums for my daily use in buying the things that bring me and my family pleasure and security.*

TREASURE NO. 6—YOUR CREATIVE IMAGINATION TO CHANGE LIFE SITUATIONS

Someone has rightly said, "The imagination is God's workshop."

The use of your creative imagination can free you from life's burdens and problems and cause you to grow wings of the soul and rise above the gravity pull of earth.

Your imagination is a creative mystical power which can take the raw elements of life and forge them into tools that carve out a perfect destiny.

Sit in daily periods of meditation for the next few weeks and practice using this mystic power of the creative imagination.

MEDITATION TO STRENGTHEN THE POWER OF IMAGINATION

Use the following meditation to strengthen this power of your creative imagination:

I now dwell in the mystic realm of my higher creative imagination. I create in the image and likeness of the mental patterns that I call up from my imagination. I see myself healthy and happy. I project money and all the good things of life. I dwell in thoughts of happiness, love fulfillment and friendship with other people. I am mentally serene and calm and project myself into situations that are peaceful and harmonious.

Testimony No. 55

Howard R. Used the Power of Imagination to Become Factory Foreman

Howard R. was in a factory job where he tended a punch press. He had little formal education, and it seemed to be the only type of work that he could do. Howard had learned how to project his imaginative patterns of thought through our class lessons and he began to project each night, when he went to bed, the imaginative picture of himself being made foreman of the factory. This seemed an impossible dream at the time, but his boss soon began to notice that Howard was a careful, hard worker. He began giving him little extra jobs with more responsibility. When one of the big punch presses broke down one day, Howard had it working again in a short time; he seemed to have an instinct for machinery.

A few months later, when the foreman of the factory retired, as a result of an illness, it was Howard that the owner put into the foreman's position! His salary was nearly doubled, his work was easier and Howard had proof that his creative imagination had power to bring him his new-found success.

TREASURE NO. 7—PLEASURE
DERIVED FROM YOUR EMOTIONS

Without the pleasure that you derive from your emotions, do you realize that life would be lived practically on the level of a vegetable or a low form of animal life?

You can experience a rich emotional life that brings you joy and beauty, through the emotions that you feel and express.

A good meditation to use for daily exercise of your positive emotions is the following:

> *I am aware of the transforming power of my positive emotions. I now pass the emotion of faith through the prism of my higher mind, and it changes my life into a brilliant mosaic of life experiences that reflect this divine emotion. I have faith in God, faith in myself and in the brilliant destiny that is being fashioned for me through God's Tapestry of Dreams.*
>
> *I now attune my mind and soul to the cosmic wavelengths of Truth, Good, Love, Beauty, Joy and Peace and my life becomes a glorious pageant of fulfillment of my every dream.*

TREASURE NO. 8—THE FIVE SENSES WHICH MAKE YOU AWARE OF LIFE'S BLESSINGS

You have been given your five senses to make you aware of the world in which you live, so you can enjoy all the blessings of life.

MEDITATION TO USE FOR INCREASING LIFE ENJOYMENT THROUGH THE FIVE SENSES

Use the following meditation to give you awareness of your five senses:

> *I am aware of the gift of sight, in which I view a world of miracles. I thank God for my eyes and perfect vision. I now see the world as being beautiful and I am aware of all the hidden treasures that are in the beauty of nature, the secrets behind the universe and the mystery of God.*
>
> *I am now aware of my ability to hear the singing of birds, the whispering of the wind through towering tree tops, the hushed murmuring of ocean waves gently kissing the seashore. I listen to the sounds of children's happy laughter and love's muted harmony, and I am attuned to the cosmic music of the spheres.*
>
> *I know the world around me through the sense of feeling, and I respond to the touch of fragrant rose petals, the gentle falling of rain upon the soft earth, the downy touch of snowflakes upon my cheeks,*

the caress of a lover's hand upon my brow, and of a child's trusting hand clasped in mine.
I contact the soul of the universe through prayer and meditation and I am rewarded by the gentle flow of spirit as it caresses my heart and soul with its sweet promise of peace and love.

I am aware of the fragrance of orange blossoms in full bloom and myriad fields of flowers that waft their perfume to my senses. I drink in the sweet profusion of intoxicating fragrances and I know that these delights have been created for my enjoyment.

I partake of the festive board of life with its many savory delights and my taste buds are satiated daily with a variety of good things produced by mother nature for my delectation. I am grateful for this everflowing, copious stream of nourishing products that give me life and joy.

I am in touch with a throbbing, vibrant, beautiful universe that reveals itself through my five senses and I am enriched by the manifold blessings that have been showered upon me by a loving Creator.

TREASURE NO. 9—PEACE OF MIND AND PEACE OF SOUL

It is interesting to note that two of the best sellers of the past generation were two books titled: *Peace of Mind* and *Peace of Soul*. This shows that millions of people are searching for these priceless treasures today more than ever before.

In ancient mysticism, there is an exercise called Samyama, which you can use to bring you peace of mind and peace of soul.

Samyama literally means transferring the quality or virtue of an object to one's own mind, body or spirit.

Following are the exercises for making Samyama for peace of mind and peace of soul. Sit in meditation and mentally visualize a quiet lake in the countryside. Read the following statement to take on the quality of peace and tranquility that lake represents:

My mind becomes as tranquil and still as that lake. My soul now reflects the tranquility of the canopy of blue sky and golden sun. I feel a deep sense of serenity and joy within my heart and soul. There are no ripples on my mental and spiritual lake. If there are worries, fear and anxiety, these produce waves on my mental lake and I now push these ripples down into the body of the lake until it is once again smooth, still and quiescent. I am peaceful. I am tranquil and calm.

Testimony No. 56

Pamela S. Changed Into a Beautiful Swan With This Exercise

Pamela S. was considered a very plain and awkward young lady by all her friends. At parties she sat alone, seldom being asked for a dance. When she came into our work and learned these mystical and spiritual laws, she told me that she was lonely and not in love with anyone, although she was then twenty-eight years of age. She told me she felt clumsy and awkward; her features were not well-spaced or beautiful and she felt inferior and miserable.

I gave her this mystical exercise for making Samyama on beauty and grace and told her that when she walked into a room, she should visualize a field of fragrant, beautiful flowers swaying in a gentle breeze. She was to make Samyama on the beauty and grace of those flowers. Then I told her to make Samyama on the mystical and romantic aura of the full silvery moon, walking in a magic circle of silvery light. She was to visualize this magnetic aura of the moon, suffusing her face and body with the moon's magnetism and romance. By doing this exercise, she would be automatically overcoming the effects of self-consciousness and inferiority. By thinking of flowers, trees and a silvery moon, she would take on the qualities represented by these forces in nature and become graceful and charming. Her inner soul's beauty was thus released, and when people saw her, they did not see the physical part alone, but they became aware of a transcendental beauty that illumined her face and body and made her seem to be beautiful. She changed from the proverbial ugly duckling into the graceful swan overnight.

I have known many movie stars in Hollywood, especially women, who became famous because they were able to build this illusion of beauty even though their features were not always arranged symmetrically. A few of these were Katherine Hepburn, Bette Davis,

Lauren Bacall, Claudette Colbert, Sophia Loren, Greta Garbo and in more recent times, Barbra Streisand.

TREASURE NO. 10—THE SOUL'S DIVINE ORIGIN AND ONENESS WITH GOD

In mystic philosophy, we learn that the entire purpose of existence is a spiritual one, in which the soul must be aware of its divine origin and strive to blend with the soul of the universe, which reflects God.

This priceless treasure is one of consciousness, rather than any specific material or physical thing. It can only be achieved through a process of mystic contemplation and meditation.

The ancients often referred to the lowly caterpillar as an example of man's gradual metamorphosis from an earth-bound creature to one who grows wings of the soul and ascends into the spiritual stratosphere of eternality and glory.

As the caterpillar contains within its crawling, earth-bound self the image of the multi-colored butterfly that will one day emerge, so too, man possesses within his earth-bound, physical self, the soul that will one day cause him to ascend to the spiritual state known as Bodhisattvahood in the Tantric Mysticism of Tibet.

MEDITATION TO ACHIEVE BLENDING WITH THE LIGHT

In the following meditation you will contemplate on this divine mystery that frees your soul from the Karmic wheel of fate, so it may complete its journey into the state of Bodhisattvahood, or blending with the light.

I now contemplate the mystery that is behind my life. I am a part of the pulsating rhythm of cosmic harmony which is represented by the soul of the universe. I now blend with this cosmic power which elevates me to spiritual heights.

I take on the virtue of infinite good and the mystic chord of goodness now vibrates within my mind, body and soul, causing me to do good, be good and respond to good. I take on the virtue of infinite peace and this mystic chord now vibrates in my life, bringing harmony with those around me and banishing all discord and friction.

MYSTO-MATIC POINTERS

If you wish to actually achieve material riches and abundance you can still use this complete method given above for finding the other mental, emotional and spiritual treasures of life.

You can now add to this mystical method the seven mystical chords of cosmic money magnetism and meditate each day on these seven rays of mystic power to bring you riches.

1. *Desire. Sit in meditation and hold your mind on the things that you wish to attract with intense desire.*

2. *Build money awareness by contemplating the reality of money; see it as spiritual energy released in creative acts.*

3. *Use the mystic power of Mental Alchemy to turn your ideas into gold. A thought is as real as a skyscraper or bridge. In your mind's eye see your ideas turn into gold. Meditate on the reality of the things you wish to create in your life, such as owning your home, driving a beautiful car, having expensive furnishings and clothing, jewels, lands and other things of value. These thoughts help release the mental alchemy that can translate your ideas into things of value.*

4. *Invoke the law of cosmic magnetism which states that money goes to money, nothing succeeds like success, birds of a feather flock together. You will attract that which you most often hold in consciousness. Magnetize money by having some useful purpose in life for which you need money. Have a desire to help educate your children, to better the world, to banish war. These cosmic motivations help increase your money magnetism.*

5. *Utilize the law of reciprocity to help you attract money and money equivalents. This law is stated in the bible: As ye sow, so shall ye reap. Are you giving something to the world of value for which you expect money rewards? If*

not, then learn something you can do which makes your
work valuable to others and release this to the world. You
will be rewarded in accordance to your own value to
others.

6. Use the law of imagination to project money into your
   life. See yourself in work you enjoy doing, earning big
   money. See your own business with employees helping
   you make a fortune. Imagination is one of the mystical
   chords to cosmic magnetism.

7. Use the positive emotion of faith to release the creative
   energy of your higher mind centers. Have faith in
   yourself, have faith in your great destiny and have faith in
   God.

14

MYSTERIES OF THE
I CHING UNVEIL
YOUR FUTURE
DESTINY

The ancient Chinese mystics designed a method for determining future events which they called the I Ching. They believed that Fate could point out Tao or the Way, through the divine law of Causation.

They taught that the Soul's Karmic Birthpath was preordained and that a person could learn of certain events that would transpire in his life by aligning his mind with the forces of Fate.

These mystics prepared lists of questions which could be asked by the person wanting to know his future, then they tossed a few short sticks which fell into various patterns they called hexagrams. By interpreting these designs, they could accurately foretell certain events that were destined to befall them. A long list of questions and answers were prepared in advance and the various patterns produced by tossing the sticks determined which answers applied to the questions asked.

Sometimes coins were used by the ancient Chinese to point out the pattern of events. However, I have adapted this system of I Ching to our modern usage and simplified it greatly. Instead of using sticks or coins to determine the answers to the questions asked, I have substituted dice to show the way or Tao for the unfolding of the future destiny.

The toss of the dice is left entirely in the hands of Fate and the six sides of the dice give a wide enough variety of answers to our questions to suit modern needs.

QUESTIONS CHOSEN FROM LIFE'S
25 MOST COMMON EXPERIENCES

There are twenty-five typical life experiences given below. You may choose any of these questions and the answers will be preordained by the fall of the dice, which will give you the answer to the question you ask. You may ask one or more questions at any one sitting, in any of the twenty-five categories given.

The throw of the dice, determined by the law of cause and effect, would be considered by the ancient Chinese mystics, as a preordained psychic evaluation or revelation of the events that are to occur in the present or the future.

LIST OF QUESTIONS

1. Will I succeed in my present business venture?
2. Will I get the sum of money that I expect?
3. Will this problem be solved in my favor?
4. Should I change my residence at this time?
5. Should I marry this person?
6. Will I have children in my marriage?
7. Will I take the trip I plan?
8. Can I trust this person?
9. Will I be able to overcome this illness?

10. Will I make a fortune in my lifetime?
11. Will this gambling venture prove successful?
12. How will this legal problem turn out?
13. Will I inherit money from any source?
14. Will this person recover from this illness?
15. Will I ever become rich?
16. Can I succeed in the stock market?
17. Should I sell this property at this time?
18. Does the person I love really love me?
19. Will I locate my missing valuables?
20. Will I live a long, healthy life?
21. Will I get the job I want?
22. Should I ask for a raise in salary at this time?
23. How can I win the love of this person?
24. Should I try to go into my own business?
25. Should I go through with plans for a divorce?

INSTRUCTIONS FOR USING I CHING TO PREDICT YOUR FUTURE

1. First, select your question or questions from the list of twenty-five questions that are given above. You may select more than one question, as each throw of the dice will reveal the suitable course of action that you should take, according to the nature of your questions.

2. Now take one dice only and roll it. As there are six numbers on the dice there will be six possible answers to your questions.

3. After you obtain the number from the dice which will give you the answer to your question, turn to the category in which your question falls and the number designated by the dice will be given. That will be the answer to that particular question.

For example, if you asked question number one, "Will I succeed in my present business venture?" and you roll the dice and it comes up number three, then you turn to number three under the section dealing with business. The answer will be: Be cautious, especially if this is a partnership. Something will happen to disrupt your plans and bring about a sudden decision to abandon this project in favor of something else.

Following are the various answers given for the different questions asked.

QUESTION #1: WILL I SUCCEED IN
MY PRESENT BUSINESS VENTURE?

1. Yes, you will succeed, this is basically a good venture but will require a great deal of patience to make it a success.

2. There is a possibility of two courses of action; one depends on assistance from another person; the other, on whether you have sufficient money to close this deal at present.

3. Be cautious, especially if this is a partnership. Something will happen to disrupt your plans and bring about a sudden decision to abandon this project in favor of something else.

4. There are apt to be several delays and disappointments in this business venture. It will not completely fulfill your expectations. Adopt a wait and see attitude.

5. You are now in a cycle of changes and important decisions, so hold off action for a while longer. You will receive a definite go ahead signal when the time is ripe.

6. It is too risky a venture at this time. It is better to give up this venture and wait for a more opportune time to carry out such a plan.

QUESTION #2: WILL I GET THE
SUM OF MONEY THAT I EXPECT?

1. The money you expect will come to you in the designated time. Use it wisely to secure your future and avoid spending it on unnecessary things.

2. There are doubts that you will receive this money that you expect. Some person is holding up payment and you may have to take further action to obtain it in the specified time.

3. Be careful not to complicate matters by taking action that might be offensive or threatening. Wait and see if the money does not come through a natural course of events.

4. A period of frustrations and delays is apt to occur in regard to money

matters. Seek an alternative course through a bank loan or some person you know who can assist you.

5. Your life situation appears to be changing. Money will be slow in coming and you can expect small amounts to meet your current needs. Do not give up plans to increase your income.

6. Do not depend on this source for the sum of money you desire. There is a danger that your financial condition will rapidly deteriorate unless you take definite steps to cut down on expenses and limit your risks in investments or business.

QUESTION #3: WILL THIS PROBLEM BE SOLVED IN MY FAVOR?

1. A solution to your problem is definitely on the way. It will materialize suddenly and it will definitely prove favorable to you.

2. There are two possible solutions: One depends on another person's help, and the other on the timing. Be patient and wait.

3. Be careful not to settle on a partial solution as there is danger the persons involved will try to trick you in some way.

4. A time element is involved in this problem that must be carefully worked out. Take active steps to remove obstacles.

5. If you sit back and relax, having done all you can, this problem will solve itself in this cycle of changes for the better.

6. Be careful not to sign legal papers or put too much faith in the word of a person who may deceive you. You are in a period of risks and dangers and must use caution.

QUESTION #4: SHOULD I CHANGE MY RESIDENCE AT THIS TIME?

1. Yes, you will change your residence at this time. You have outlived your purpose in the present home and it is time to change.

2. The issue is clouded; a change may be desirable, but you will find it difficult to make the move under present conditions.

3. Don't jump from the frying pan into the fire; look over the new place carefully to be sure it meets all your needs.

4. A delay is shown in your plans to move. It may not be easy to find the

type of place you desire. It might be better to put this move off until a better time.

5. As you are in a new cycle at this time, a change in residence is favored. Start to make plans now, and they will mature soon.

6. There are risks involved in making this move at present. Avoid taking on debts, and be sure that the neighborhood is right before making a change.

QUESTION #5: SHOULD I MARRY
THIS PERSON?

1. It is indicated that this person would be a suitable mate. You have a great deal in common and can build a good marriage.

2. There will be conflict within your mind, for you will have a choice between two persons that you seem to love equally.

3. Many hidden dangers exist in this romance. Look at your future in-laws and ask if you could be happy in such a marriage.

4. A period of delays and frustrations is shown in love at present. Do not be disappointed if your plans fall through at the last minute.

5. A romantic affair ends and a new one begins with a person you have recently met. Continue with this person until you are sure.

6. At best, this would turn out to be a temporary marriage filled with problems and disappointments. You can do better by waiting.

QUESTION #6: WILL I HAVE
CHILDREN IN MY MARRIAGE?

1. A family of two children is indicated; a boy and a girl who will be born two years apart. They will be healthy and normal.

2. Owing to a difficult time financially it may be necessary for you to wait a year or two before having children.

3. There may be problems in having a natural childbirth. Check into this carefully and if you cannot have natural children you may consider adopting some.

4. Marriage problems that arise owing to difficulties with in-laws make it advisable to think twice before having children.

5. Three children will bless your union, but many home changes may make it difficult to rear them with security.

6. The possibility of incompatibility with your mate and the chance for the marriage to end in divorce make it inadvisable to have children in this union.

QUESTION #7: WILL I TAKE THE TRIP I PLAN?

1. Yes, you will take this trip, and it will bring you pleasure and relaxation. A romantic episode will occur that brings happiness.

2. There is a strong possibility you will have to wait a while before taking this trip, owing to some financial problems.

3. Some business matters may require attention first. After this is taken care of, you will take this trip and enjoy it.

4. There will be several delays in your plans to take a trip at this time. Unexpected problems will arise, causing you to defer it.

5. A very important business matter arises that may make it necessary for you to put it off for at least six more months.

6. If you take this trip, there will be disappointments that make it most unpleasant. Do not take chances at this time.

QUESTION #8: CAN I TRUST THIS PERSON?

1. Proceed with plans already made, and have confidence that this person will prove trustworthy and helpful.

2. Limit your activities with this person, and do not put too much trust in the entire situation. Avoid a long relationship.

3. If you are involved in a money deal with this person, try not to put too much faith or trust in this person.

4. A period of mutual trust will be followed by a bitter disappointment in something that this person will do to you.

5. The person means well, but there are other factors involved that may bring about a radical change in your future plans.

6. Terminate this contact, or it will cause you loss of money and time. You will find someone else who can assist you.

QUESTION #9: WILL I BE ABLE TO
OVERCOME THIS ILLNESS?

1. Improvement is shown quickly, so avoid being unduly alarmed. Follow your doctor's advice implicitly and all will be well.

2. It may be necessary to continue with medication for some time, as this health problem may be the result of past neglect.

3. Avoid self-medication for this condition, as it might develop into something serious. Consult your family physician.

4. A temporary health difficulty is shown that will respond to rest, diet and mild exercise.

5. Congestion and inflammation will subside quickly with plenty of rest and by maintaining a cheerful mental attitude.

6. A brief illness is indicated that will leave you in good physical condition, but weak for a time. Take better care of yourself in the future.

QUESTION #10: WILL I MAKE A
FORTUNE IN MY LIFETIME?

1. The potential to make a fortune in the future is there within your mind. This will be through creative ideas.

2. A long term investment in real estate could bring you a fortune over a period of several years. Begin to invest now.

3. Avoid speculations in gold, oil or stocks. Stick with the tried and tested in a business that you know, and you will be rich in the future.

4. After a few futile starts, you will hit on an idea that can make you a fortune in the next ten years. Spend it wisely.

5. Avoid gambling and speculation if you wish to become rich. Your fortunes will fluctuate and vary throughout your lifetime.

6. You are on a rocky financial course that can spell disaster. Build a new sense of values and develop more money awareness.

QUESTION #11: WILL THIS
GAMBLING VENTURE PROVE
SUCCESSFUL?

1. You are in a lucky cycle that can bring you financial rewards through games of chance.

2. Your natural timidity about losing money makes it doubtful if you can ever become a successful gambler. Give it up.

3. Use caution in all gambling ventures. Do it only for fun, occasionally, and never for more than you can afford.
4. You will win just enough money to tempt you to go back and lose what you won. It is better to stay away from gambling.
5. Your luck will change suddenly, and after a period of losses you will begin to hit a lucky streak. Quit when you're ahead.
6. Yours is not a lucky fate when it comes to gambling. You will risk losing everything if you indulge this habit.

QUESTION #12: HOW WILL THIS LEGAL PROBLEM TURN OUT?

1. Trust your lawyer, as you are in good hands, and you will win out in this case after a seeming reversal.
2. Through mistakes made by your opponents, you still have a very good chance of coming out on top in this legal problem.
3. Be careful not to say something on the witness stand that will be apt to prejudice your case. It does not look too good now.
4. Just when everything seems lost, the scales of justice will tip in your favor and bring you an unexpected settlement.
5. A sudden shift of tactics by the opposing attorney could bring you an unexpected victory and a good settlement.
6. Try to settle this matter out of court as there is grave danger that the verdict could go against you.

QUESTION #13: WILL I INHERIT MONEY FROM ANY SOURCE?

1. A change in a person's will has already been made that assures you of getting a sizable inheritance when that person dies.
2. Some member of the family may be jealous of you and make underhanded efforts to have your name removed from a will.
3. Proceed with your friendship with this person of wealth, as there is a very real possibility that you will be left money.
4. An elderly person with a substantial fortune is being urged to name you in a will. A change in the will could occur soon.
5. Plans to give you an inheritance may be altered by a person who is not yet convinced of your worthiness to receive benefits.
6. Do not waste time and money on a wealthy person, for it is doubtful if a legacy will ever be left for you in this person's will.

Testimony No. 57

Sara L. Consulted the I Ching About a Will and Received $150,000

Sara L. was estranged from her wealthy father through the malicious gossip of her brother. Sara was living in New York City and her family lived in Kansas City. Her mother was dead and her father had a stroke that left him partially paralyzed. He had to go about in a wheel chair. As her father had a fortune of more than a quarter of a million dollars, Sara became quite concerned about being left out of his will when he died.

Upon learning our system for consulting the I Ching, she asked question no. 13, WILL I INHERIT MONEY FROM ANY SOURCE? She rolled the dice and number two came up; she consulted the answer under number two and it said, "Some member of the family may be jealous of you and make underhanded efforts to have your name removed from a will."

Then Sara asked question #2: WILL I GET THE SUM OF MONEY I EXPECT. She rolled the dice and Number 1 came up, which said, "The money you expect will come to you in the designated time. Use it wisely to secure your future and avoid spending it on unnecessary things."

These two answers convinced Sara that she must take some positive steps to assure her that the father would remember her in his will. She wrote her father a long, conciliatory letter and wound up by asking him if he would come to New York City and visit her. He telephoned her upon receiving her letter and said he would be happy to visit her. He arrived in New York, and she met him at the plane. Although he was in a wheel chair, Sara was able to take him to see the various museums and galleries, they visited the opera and had many happy hours together. Before leaving New York, Sara's father confessed that he had changed his will, owing to her brother's pressure, but now that he had seen her again, he was changing the will back to its original form, giving her a large share of his estate when he died.

A year later Sara's father died and upon the settling of the will, she received the sum of $150,000!

QUESTION #14: WILL THIS PERSON
RECOVER FROM THIS ILLNESS?

1. A complete recovery is indicated but the person will have to use great care in the future not to have a recurrence of illness.

2. If the doctor's instructions are carefully followed, this person has a good chance of recovering without any future ill effects.

3. The doctor may suggest a rather drastic treatment that could include an operation. Follow the doctor's advice.

4. After a brief period of uncertainty, the patient will begin to make a complete recovery, but it will be a long, slow process.

5. It may be necessary to consult another doctor in this case. Delays and obstacles seem to occur that should be checked into.

6. There is grave danger that recovery will not be complete and that the patient may have a relapse that will prove serious.

QUESTION #15: WILL I EVER
BECOME RICH?

1. With your shrewd mind and creative thinking, there is every likelihood that you will become rich sometime in middle age.

2. If you use your creative intelligence and go into your own business, there is a chance for you to have a big income throughout your life.

3. You will make and lose two fortunes through your own carelessness. Strive to use caution in your business dealings and avoid gambling.

4. After a period of losses and delays, you will suddenly have a spurt of good luck that could take you to financial independence.

5. There are many financial changes on the horizon for you. Stick with your present business plans, and you will have financial independence, but not great wealth in the future.

6. The present course of action will lead you into financial problems that are apt to mitigate against your ever being wealthy.

QUESTION #16: CAN I SUCCEED IN
THE STOCK MARKET?

1. By a careful study of the financial picture at this time, you can safely invest in the stock market and have substantial profits.

2. Avoid investing more than you can afford. As the market will fluctuate drastically in the months ahead, you must study conditions carefully before investing your money.

3. The indications are not too favorable for you to have success in this type of speculation. You would be better in your own business.

4. After a period of some profits in the stock market, you will hit a losing cycle. It is better to get out than continue to lose.

5. Change your financial picture, and vary your investments. The stock market does not seem the most favorable source for future wealth.

6. Your type of temperament cannot stand the uncertainty of the stock market, so avoid taking chances in this difficult field.

QUESTION #17: SHOULD I SELL
THIS PROPERTY AT THIS TIME?

1. By disposing of this property now, you will have an opportunity to use the money you receive for a more lucrative investment.

2. An offer may come that you will consider, but at the last moment, the deal is apt to fall through. Keep trying until you succeed.

3. The real estate market is going through a radical change. It will be wise for you to wait until property values rise.

4. There are indications that you will be forced to wait a while longer before you are able to dispose of this property.

5. You have a three-month period ahead of you in which profits are shown in real estate. Take action in that time to sell.

6. Get rid of this property now, and do not wait for it to improve in value, as you face a declining financial cycle.

QUESTION #18: DOES THE PERSON
I LOVE REALLY LOVE ME?

1. You can be sure that this person does love you. At times, there may be actions that show carelessness, but there is real love here.

2. There are some doubts regarding this romance. You should not make serious plans for a permanent union until you know for sure.

3. A character weakness makes it difficult for you to ever really get along with this person. Search elsewhere for your true soul mate.

4. This romance will be an on-again-off-again type that will sorely test your patience. You deserve someone much better.

5. Two people you met recently may profess love for you. Test them both for a while before you make any decisions in love.

6. A doubtful romance that will bring problems. It should end as amicably as possible. Look for someone more compatible to you.

QUESTION #19: WILL I LOCATE MY MISSING VALUABLES?

1. You will locate your missing valuables as you calm down and let your subconscious mind guide you to where they are misplaced.

2. There are several factors involved that make it somewhat doubtful if you will locate them. Another person is apt to be involved and this could be a suspicious circumstance.

3. Avoid hysteria and calmly sit down and trace your actions preceding the loss. It is likely they have been temporarily misplaced and will be located soon.

4. After a period of time you will discover that the valuables were put in a place where it was assumed they were safe. A recovery of these valuables is likely, after some delays.

5. Search for the valuables in places that you would be least likely to look. There is a chance they have been taken and placed in a box where you thought they would be safe.

6. There is little likelihood that you will discover these lost valuables. Some person is involved in the disappearance.

QUESTION #20: WILL I LIVE A LONG, HEALTHY LIFE?

1. After some minor illnesses, you will gain in strength and should live a long, healthy and prosperous life.

2. You can live longer than your life expectation by being careful to avoid bad habits such as smoking and drinking.

3. A careful diet and the avoidance of excess weight will be the two key factors in your living your natural life span. Begin now to keep your diet in control and get plenty of rest and exercise.

4. Many of your health problems will be the result of stress situations in your life. To live long, avoid worry, fear and hate.

5. You are going through a profound mental and physical change which will affect your health and give you a longer life.

6. The course you are now on is apt to shorten your life expectancy. Change your style of living, rest more and avoid rich foods (particularly starches and carbohydrates).

QUESTION #21: WILL I GET THE JOB THAT I WANT?

1. You are in line for a very interesting and lucrative position that will bring you every reward you expect from your work.
2. An improvement is shown in your working conditions, but it is not the best thing that you could attract. Try for something that brings you easier working conditions and more money.
3. After a period of uncertainty in your work you will find it necessary to make a change. However, wait until the time is ready.
4. Through some friend, you will learn of an opening in a place where you could find work that is suitable to your talents.
5. Make the change as quickly as possible, for you are working too hard for too little money in your present job.
6. It is not a good time to make this business change. Stay where you are until you have built up a financial backlog, then change.

QUESTION #22: SHOULD I ASK FOR A RAISE IN SALARY AT THIS TIME?

1. Your chances of obtaining a raise in salary at this time are excellent. Know your true worth and don't be afraid to ask.
2. The company may not be willing to give you that raise in salary owing to heavy overhead, so put this off for a while.
3. Be prepared to give up your job and try to find one more worthy of your talents, because the salary raise you expect will not be forthcoming.
4. Wait until better times are indicated in business before you ask for a raise in salary. You may be worth it, but the boss may not be able to grant your wishes in this matter.
5. You are long overdue for this raise and you should ask for it, even though it may not be granted at this time.
6. Avoid confrontation with your employer at this time over a salary

raise. It is not apt to be granted and could cause a crisis in your relationship.

QUESTION #23: HOW CAN I WIN
THE LOVE OF THIS PERSON?

1. Be your own natural, charming self, and you will easily win the love and attention of the person you have chosen.
2. A romantic change is indicated for you but first there must be a winding up of an old romance that could stand in your way.
3. Be more aggressive and let this person you love know that you desire a permanent relationship and you will be on the way to it.
4. No matter what you do, there are obstacles in the way of this romance that make it impossible for this person to really fall in love with you. Seek out some other person.
5. Don't grieve if this person does not respond to you, for you deserve someone who really appreciates your qualities and true beauty of soul.
6. This person may respond to your overtures and show some emotional reaction, but it is apt to be false and will soon end.

QUESTION #24: SHOULD I TRY TO
GO INTO MY OWN BUSINESS?

1. This is an excellent time for you to take a firm step in the direction of having your own business. The money will come, so be firm in your resolve.
2. If you have a partner who is willing to meet you halfway, you should consider taking this step at the present time.
3. There are obstacles that stand in your way at present. It would be better for you to have more capital for this venture.
4. Stay in your present business endeavor, for the time is not yet ripe for you to embark upon such a speculative venture.
5. Start to make plans for going into your own business in the next two or three years by preparing yourself financially.
6. Avoid taking on such a responsibility. You are better off working for a salary until such time as you show your ability to branch out for yourself.

QUESTION #25: SHOULD I GO
THROUGH WITH PLANS FOR A
DIVORCE?

1. You have done everything you can to avoid this break-up of your marriage. Now, you must carry through with your plans.

2. After many false starts and new beginnings, you are now convinced that this person is not capable of changing, so use your own good judgment as to whether you should break it up.

3. Some other person may try to interfere in this marriage and cause your mate to act in a strange and hostile manner.

4. There seems no other way out of your difficult situation. If you wish to delay this divorce for a while, because of conditions in the home, do so; ultimately, you must act.

5. A new romantic partner will finally force you to take the steps in winning your freedom that you have long desired.

6. Be sure that you obtain the right financial settlement before you go through with this action. Better to end it than continue in disharmony for many more painful years.

MYSTO-MATIC POINTERS

1. *You can use your own variations to the questions given in the prepared list. For instance you may ask a question about litigation over a will, and you can use Question number 12, but word it differently: Will I win out in the court case about the will? Any other questions you ask should be put into the various categories given of life's 25 most common problems.*

2. *In using I Ching, remember that you are still a person of "free will," and if the answer does not seem to conform to your own desires, you can still act contrary to the advice given.*

3. *Use I Ching as a guiding force, rather than a decisive force; if the answer is what you expected, it will give you greater courage to act accordingly. If opposite to your*

  expectations, you must work harder to make the project a success.

4. You can use the I Ching as a parlor game, giving enjoyment to friends and family, even if the answers may not be taken seriously.

5. As the original Oriental I Ching was used to advise noble persons in ancient courts, most of the terms in past I Ching books are intended for such special occasions. These have been formulated to fit our modern 20th Century.

6. As the toss of the dice is left to chance, you can readily assume that nothing is predetermined in fate, but a situation may turn either way, for or against you. Work with fate when possible.

15

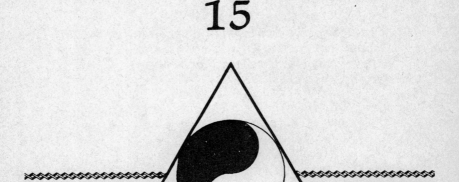

TAKE THE CELESTIAL JOURNEY OF THE SOUL THROUGH ASTRAL PROJECTION

Astral projection can be achieved by anyone who learns this method from the ancient lands of Tibet and India. The soul is now known to be a reality that has form and dimension, and which can leave the body under controlled conditions while you sleep. The soul has its final separation from the body in the last stage of life, which is really a rebirth into a completely new dimension of existence that is spiritual rather than physical.

Your soul is the divine antenna that attunes you to the soul of the universe.

From the pulsating rhythms of this cosmic spirit, which is the emanation from the divine source of life which we call God, you can directly receive revelations while you sleep; you can be guided by Masters of the Astral realms, who can show you how to do great things, even as they did while on earth; you can visit the past recorded sites of history and learn many important events which can help you in this lifetime. On the Astral realms, at night, as your soul reaches back into time and space, you can read the Akashic record of the past and even project your soul into the future realms and know the events scheduled for that other dimension of time and space that will be occupied by your soul.

PROOF THAT THE SOUL IS A REALITY

At last, modern science now has proof that the soul is a reality. In France, scientists weighed a man at the exact moment that death occurred and found that the body became a few ounces lighter when his soul left the body at death.

But, more startling still, are photographs taken with infra-red rays at the time a person died; it was shown in the photographs that a luminous, cloud-like material rose from the body, exactly the size and shape of the physical body, at the moment death occurred!

The mystical realm of sleep is very often where the phenomenon of astral projection occurs. Dreams are sometimes very vivid, giving life-like colors, sounds and dimensions in which the dreamer is caught up in the action as it transpires. Sometimes, these dreams are astral projections in which the soul is reliving certain events of past incarnations, and many times, the dreams are prophetic astral projections of events that are still to occur.

Testimony No. 58

A Woman Had an Astral Projection of a Tragic Fire

Wanda E. had learned about Astral projection in our classes in Carnegie Hall some years ago. Her husband was a traveling salesman who was on the road several weeks at a time. One night Wanda had a vivid astral dream of a raging fire in a big hotel. She saw the vivid red flames, she heard the screams of people who seemed to be jumping out of windows to their deaths; she awakened with a stifled feeling, hardly able to breathe. Her husband happened to be home that night and she awakened him, telling him of her vivid, frightening dream. He told her to go back to sleep, that it was only a dream, a nightmare that had no reality to it.

Three weeks later her husband happened to be on a sales trip to Atlanta, Georgia. He stopped at a famous hotel, and retired for the night. Some hours later he awakened and thought he smelled smoke. He remembered his wife's dream, so he got up instantly, put on his clothes and walked down four flights of stairs to the street. The hotel was indeed on fire, and later, many hundreds of people were trapped on the upper floors; some leaped to their deaths, exactly as Wanda had seen this tragic event portrayed in her prophetic astral dream!

REGIMEN FOR ACHIEVING
ASTRAL PROJECTION WHILE YOU
SLEEP

1. When you go to bed at night tell yourself that you are going to utilize those eight hours or more of sleep to take astral journeys and learn priceless secrets from the Masters on other planes.

2. Do not be afraid to try Astral projection for fear that your soul may not return to your body. Your soul will never leave your body accidentally while on the astral, for your soul is tied to your body by a golden spiritual umbilical cord, very much like a child is tied to its mother by a physical umbilical cord. Your soul cannot permanently leave your body until the spiritual rebirth occurs, which sends it on to other dimensions of time and space. Astral projection is exactly what the term implies: It is the projection of your soul to other realms for brief periods of time while you sleep.

INSTRUCT YOUR SOUL TO REVEAL
THE AKASHIC RECORD OF YOUR
PAST

3. You can instruct your soul before you take astral flights, that you wish to remember the astral dreams and that you wish to visit certain periods of history. You can also ask it to reveal to you the Akashic record that is your soul's former lives, who you were, what you did, and what your birth karma will be in this lifetime.

4. To prepare yourself for astral projection while you sleep, lie down on

your bed in a relaxed manner, as though preparing for normal sleep. Slow down the rhythm of your breathing; take a deep inhalation, hold it for a few moments, and then exhale slowly. When you have achieved a rhythmic, slow breathing, you can begin the process of exteriorization or projection of your soul. You can think: I now command my soul to ascend to the astral realms. where I shall be given prophetic visions of my future destiny. I ask for guidance from the Illumined Masters, who will reveal secrets of the universe and impart wisdom and knowledge that I can use in this world. I wish to read the Akashic record of my past lives, so I may better know how to work out my karmic destiny in this life.

5. As you keep inhaling deeply and slowly, let yourself feel as though you are drifting upwards. Your body will seem to have no weight, and there may be a feeling of lightness in your head, but do not be alarmed, as this is perfectly natural. Then, you may feel a tugging in the middle of your body, where the diaphragm is located. As you exteriorize the soul you may begin to feel a spiraling motion, as though you are soaring up and out of your body.

At this time, you may drift into a state of unconsciousness where you will hear beautiful music or see swirling colors like a thousand rainbows. Many people report that when they achieve this first astral projection they see a golden light, that is celestial in its intensity, and then they seem to be floating up, like an airplane, at a dizzying pace. Sometimes they have looked back and have seen their bodies, at other times, they are aware of floating in space, like a rocket ship propelling a space craft to the moon, and they are aware of millions of stars and moons, in a kaleidoscope of color, against a deep purple night sky.

6. Then, after this first vivid experience, your soul may have achieved its projection into the astral realms. You will then begin to have vivid experiences, which are like dreams, except they are more vivid and intense than regular dreams.

7. It is in this phase of your astral projection that your soul will orbit into the realms of experience that are dictated by your instructions and desires. Or, your soul may find it necessary to give you an astral prophecy that can help you with some problem that you are experiencing. Many times in this phase of astral projection the soul will send back a vivid astral dream for solving a money problem or how to locate something of value.

Testimony No. 59

A Man Discovered Oil on His Farm
Through an Astral Revelation

An instance of how the soul helps one discover a fortune is seen in the experience of Wilbur T., who owned a small farm in northern Pennsylvania. He had visited New York in my early years of lecturing there, and I had told about how one could achieve astral projection and receive guidance in one's life. Wilbur was having a terrible problem making a living. His small farm was devoted to raising cattle but the cows gave little milk, for the source of their water was a small spring that had become tainted by scum-like substance that made it impossible to drink. It was in the desperate state that Wilbur made up his mind to sell his farm for whatever he could get.

That night, he decided to go into astral projection and ask his soul to discover a method for saving him from utter failure. He had a vivid astral dream, in which he floated over the area where he recognized his farm, but instead of seeing barren land in the location where the polluted springs were located, he saw towering structures which looked like oil derricks! He awakened with a start, for this was such an unlikely dream that he instantly put it down as a faulty vision.

However, out of curiosity one day, he wandered down to the springs where his cattle would no longer drink water. Something made him put his hand into the slime-covered water. He sniffed at his fingers and the scum smelled suspiciously like oil! The oil company signed a lease with Wilbur, they drilled and oil gushed in. Then they drilled on more sites and each one produced gushing oil. It was the beginning of an oil boom in that part of the country and it made Wilbur rich beyond his wildest dreams!

HOW TO INTERPRET SYMBOLS
THAT COME THROUGH ASTRAL
PROJECTION

8.   Sometimes, while you are on an astral flight you will receive dream symbols that are trying to reveal a pattern of your future destiny. Some of the most common symbols which come in astral dreams are as follows:

- A car or an airplane or train, could be telling you about a trip you are to take.
- A telephone or a letter, could be showing you that you will receive something important through the mails or phone.
- Water, if calm and peaceful, indicates that some problem in your life will be resolved satisfactorily.
- A dream of turbulent waves that bring fear could be warnings that your life will have some difficult times ahead that may upset your ship of state unless you are careful.
- A dream of walking among snakes that do not bite you could be a warning of hidden or secret enemies. Snakes or vermin crawling over the body could be warnings of some illness that will come and is a warning to get a checkup.

Testimony No. 60

An Astral Dream of Snakes Saved Joyce R's Life

Joyce R. had a recurring Astral projection that she was walking across an area where huge snakes crawled. They did not seem to harm her, but in one such astral dream one of the snakes crawled up around her chest and began to crush her breasts. She awakened, with a feeling of fear, as she could still feel some sensation where the snake seemed to have been. Because of this warning, Joyce had an examination of her breasts and an incipient tumor was found that was removed. It was cancerous and this dream may have saved her life!

To continue with the types of symbols found in astral projection:

- A thunderstorm with lightning flashing and rain pouring could be a symbolic warning of some impending disaster.
- A wedding ring is symbolic of a romantic interlude that could lead to marriage. If the wedding ring is lost or discarded or broken, it could indicate a warning in marriage.
- A long tunnel that never seems to end could indicate a period of problems that never seem to end. If there is a light at the end of the tun-

nel it could predict that you are coming to the end of a trying period in which things will improve.

- An open umbrella indicates that you will be protected or sheltered from a troublesome situation.
- Death and burial of yourself could be a warning to use caution against accidental death, or it can be a spiritual symbol of your rebirth in consciousness.
- Being locked in a coffin from which you cannot escape could be a symbol that you are imprisoned by a job or a marriage or some situation in your life that is stifling you and from which you wish to escape.
- Symbols of royalty like a crown, a throne or royal purple robes could be a flashback to a time in past incarnations when you were royalty. On the other hand, it could indicate that you wish to have the love and loyalty of those around you, which has been denied you.
- Ghosts or a haunted house with ghosts, could indicate that your mind is haunted by spectres of fear, failure, accident, sickness, poverty or death. You can then work to program your subconscious mind to get rid of these negative states of consciousness that might be making you sick, poor, unhappy and afraid.
- Guns or scenes of battle in which people are being killed could indicate that you are in a period of personal danger. You should then use extreme caution in dark places or avoid danger from strangers.
- Finding money on the street, in small or large amounts, could indicate that you are soon to be guided by your psychic mind to a venture that will bring you money financially. This could be a new business contact or an investment that produces money in the future.

Testimony No. 61

Mildred F. Found Money In Her Dreams That Led To Finding Money In Her Real Life

Mildred F. had a recurring dream in which she found various sums of money. Then, one day in an elevator she looked down and actually found a twenty dollar bill. Another time, she was caught in a terrific rainstorm, after leaving one of our classes in Carnegie Hall. She stood on the corner of 57th street and 7th avenue trying to catch a cab. Something made her look down into the swirling gutters that were filled with water. She saw something green that looked like money floating by. She reached down and grabbed it; it was a $50 bill! She later received an unexpected windfall of $35,000 from a piece of seemingly worthless property.

COMMAND AND CONTROL
OTHERS THROUGH ASTRAL
PROJECTION

9.   You can use another form of astral projection while you sleep at night. Your soul can go out into the astral realms and contact the souls of those you wish to command and control for good purposes.

"Soul speaks to soul, as star to star."

Your soul can have close communication with other souls that are on the astral realms. This is especially true if the person is someone you know or have had contact with. You can go into your astral projection sessions by giving definite instructions to your soul, such as:

While I am on the astral tonight, I wish my soul to contact J.D. and tell him that I want him to close this real estate deal at my price. He will do as I wish.

Testimony No. 62

Burt V. Commanded His Price on Some Real Estate on the Astral

This astral command was actually given by a man named Burt V. who had made an offer on a piece of property. The owner, J.D. was asking several thousand dollars more for the property. At the next meeting, without even being asked, J.D. suddenly said, "I know that this property is worth much more, but I'm going to accept your offer. If you're ready to close the deal, we can go into escrow immediately."

10. To command and control another person on the astral, when you go to bed, hold that person's face in the forefront of your mind. Then talk to the person, just as though they were there in person. Then drift off to sleep, holding in your mind the instructions you wish to give to that person on the Astral plane.

Testimony No. 63

Ruth M. Had an Astral Vision of Her Husband's Infidelity

Ruth M. had reason to believe her husband was not being true to her. She had learned about using the astral planes to reach another person, so she began to project each night when she went to bed that her soul would communicate with her husband's soul on the astral, demanding to know if her suspicions were true.

Within one week, her husband suddenly turned to her one night, as they were lying in bed, took her in his arms and kissed her. He said, "Darling, I have to confess to you that I have been having an affair with Carol. I want you to forgive me and it will never happen again." Of course, she forgave him and from that time on, she and her husband grew closer together than ever before.

HOW TO USE ASTRAL PROJECTION TO HEAL OTHER PEOPLE

11.   You can also use the astral planes to reach out and heal another person who may be at a distance from you. Scientists recently conducted tests with people that were separated by three hundred to as much as three thousand miles. One person was told to project certain thoughts that the other person's heart would begin to beat faster, or that the other person would feel sick at a certain time. The person at a distance, who was receiving these astral soul projections, actually responded exactly as directed.

Now it is found that your soul can project healing rays to friends or members of your family who may be sick and the person will respond in a very short time and become healed.

HOW TO ACCOMPLISH ASTRAL HEALING AT A DISTANCE

To accomplish this form of astral healing at a distance, when you go to bed at night, instruct your soul to go on an astral journey to the astral body of the person you wish to be healed. As you drift off into the astral, let the last thought in your mind be: "I now project my soul to the astral body of_____ (give the person's name), and I ask that that person be instantly healed. I have faith that this miracle can be accomplished, and as I sleep, the healing rays will be projected from my soul to heal the sick person."

This astral projection to the astral body of a sick person is the basis of spiritual healing which scientists cannot explain. The miracles of Lourdes for instance, where people have been cured of every known type of illness, are examples of this type of soul healing. Christ performed similar miracles by reaching into a person's soul and performing the healing.

HOW TO READ A PERSON'S AURA
ON THE ASTRAL PLANE

12. You can use soul projection for reading a person's aura, that mystical exhalation of a person's soul that reveals what the person really is. To do this, squint your eyes and look at the person. You will see a faint aura surrounding the body of the person. This aura may be blue or gold, or pink or yellow. When you have practiced for a time you can usually make out the astral color of the aura and interpret it, knowing instantly what type of person you are dealing with.

VARIOUS ASTRAL COLORS OF THE
HUMAN AURA

- An honest, highly moral person will have an aura that is sunlight yellow.
- A person who is kind and loving will have a rose colored aura.
- A person who is in creative work and artistic will have an aura that is orchid, lilac or cerulean blue.
- Someone whom you cannot trust may have a brownish tinged aura.
- A person who has some form of sickness can have an aura that is dark brown, deep blue or muddy yellow.
- A highly evolved spiritual person may have an aura that is any pastel shade from pink or yellow to light blue.

HOW TO PROJECT ASTRAL COLOR
THERAPY FOR VARIOUS TYPES OF
HEALING

13. If you should suffer from some form of illness and wish to use astral color therapy to heal yourself, you can sit in meditation and project an Astral ray to that part of the body which is afflicted.

You can use the astral colors of sunlight yellow or orange for general conditions of physical illness where there seems to be no specific cause.

For moodiness and depression, you can project the astral color of soft, viridian or nile green. You will notice that in modern hospitals the color green is used a good deal. It has been found psychologically that green has a soothing effect on the mind and nerves and makes a patient relax.

If you are trying to heal congestion of the lungs, colds, virus infections and any kind of chest condition, project the astral ray of ox-blood red.

For arthritic conditions in any part of the body project the astral ray of cerulean blue.

For stomach trouble or infections in the abdominal area, the kidneys, the excretory system or the reproductive tract, use the astral color of rosy pink.

HOW YOU CAN PROJECT ASTRAL COLOR RAYS FOR HEALING THE BODY

Sit in meditation and mentally visualize the petals of the lotus opening one by one, each having a different astral color. Now you can select the astral ray that you wish to project to that part of the body you are trying to heal with this type of meditation:

> *I now project the astral ray of deep crimson to my chest, lungs and heart. This life-giving astral ray is now removing all congestion from that area. It is stimulating my heart to beat perfectly and to be healed. My lungs now inhale and exhale the life-giving pranic force that causes them to function perfectly. I am healed, healed, healed, healed.*

If you seem to be suffering from a condition of arthritis, sit in meditation and visualize the lotus petal with the astral color of cerulean blue. Do the same meditation as above, only direct the astral ray to the specific area of the body that is afflicted.

For a general healing treatment you can use the Golden Sun projection. Visualize in the head chakra, a golden ball of light, like the sun. Now, mentally project this golden ball of light to every part of your body, starting with the head, going down into the throat, shoulders, muscles of the arms, the chest area, heart and lungs, then to the hips and the reproductive organs, and then on to the thighs, legs and feet. As you do this mental projection of the golden ball of light, you can use the following general healing meditation. If you are not sick, you can still give yourself this astral ray treatment once a day stimulate your body cells and to keep your body health:

I now project the golden ball of light to my body, for healing and to keep me healthy. I remove all impurities of every kind from my head, my chest, my abdomen, the lower parts of my body, and I now flood those areas with life-giving, restoring golden light. As the sun gives life and light to the earth, so now the cosmic golden ball of light purifies my body, renews and restores it and brings me perfect health.

MYSTO-MATIC POINTERS

1. Before going out on your Astral journeys each night, instruct your soul to give you the type of experiences you desire. Tell it, just as though talking to another person, that you wish to visit certain periods in history, or to know certain events in your past lives.

2. If you are actually having an Astral projection you will probably have vivid dreams in color. Normal dreams are usually in black and white. Events will occur in continuity in these astral dreams.

3. If your Astral projection is to a period in which you have lived before you will be an onlooker at the scene in which you will see yourself projected as the main actor in the drama you witness.

4. Make it a point to have a pencil and paper near your bed, and when you have had your astral dream, write down the events that you have participated in, for you will probably forget them before morning.

5. If you keep having the same Astral projection over and over again, there could be some event that you should know about which is leading you to some negative life Karma, so observe it carefully.

6. If, in your Astral projections, you meet people whom you have known on earth, these could be troubled souls who need guidance on the other side. Or they could be trying to point out something for you to know that may be helpful to you on this earth.

7. You can ask for Masters to guide you in Astral projection; the soul of a great composer, author, poet or inventor, could reveal vital information to help you in your own chosen career.